Agile Talent

RALF KNEGTMANS

AGILE TALENT

NINE ESSENTIAL STEPS FOR SELECTING TOMORROW'S TOP TALENT

Business Contact Publishers
Amsterdam/Antwerp

The members of the multidisciplinary think-tank deserve a resounding thank you for their part in realising this book. I was greatly inspired by their suggestions, research, feedback and advice, all of which was invaluable to the book.

Maarten van Beek – director Human Resources ING The Netherlands

Gabriëlle van Heteren – HR Business Consultant ABN AMRO Bank

Sander Klous – partner Big Data Analytics KPMG and professor Big Data Ecosystems University of Amsterdam

Jacques Kuyf – boardroom advisor, supervisory board member and partner De Vroedt & Thierry

Ylva Poelman – bionica and innovation expert, author of *De natuur als uitvinder* (only available in Dutch)

Quintin Schevernels – investor in HR technology, author of *Suits & Hoodies* (only available in Dutch)

Henk Jan Smit – partner KPMG Advisory N.V.

MIX
Papier van
verantwoorde herkomst
FSC® C004472

© 2017 Ralf Knegtmans
Business Contact Publishers
Original title *Agile talent*
Translated by Martha Osborn
Copy edited by Kevin O'Donnell
Cover and interior design Adept Vormgeving
Author photo Marc Driessen
Printer Ten Brink, Meppel
The author and publisher have made every effort to obtain permission for and acknowledge the use of copyright material. Should any infringement of copyright have occurred, please contact Business Contact Publishers.

ISBN 978 90 470 1018 0
D/2017/0108/523

www.businesscontact.nl

CORNERSTONE
INTERNATIONAL GROUP

CONTENTS

"It is not the strongest of the species that survive, nor the most intelligent, but the ones most responsive to change."

CHARLES DARWIN

PREFACE

"The illiterate of the 21ˢᵗ century will not be those that cannot read or write, but those that cannot learn, unlearn and relearn."

ALVIN TOFFLER (1928-2016)

Even as a child, talent held a particular fascination for me. Of course, I was not focused on managers, experts or leaders back then. I was intrigued by exceptional craftsmen, such as the cobbler who won European awards and displayed his trophies in his shop window. I was just as intrigued by TV celebrities and professional athletes: what was the secret of their success? Were they gifted with a special talent from birth, or did some mysterious "x factor" propel them to success? My parents had several psychologists as friends, and I would pay special attention when they discussed the topic of talent. Yet the answer to what constituted success remained elusive. My childhood musings did not lead me to the secret elixir that made some people recognisably successful, but they were a good stimulus for my later inquiries.

In 1993, I became chief operating officer of a US-based recruitment agency, and examining people's talent became part of my professional activities. I met a great many colleagues who were passionate about their field and who aimed to seek out the most talented candidates. Still, it was rarely feasible for them to research in depth every prospective job candidate, as they were often engaged in assignments from companies hit by urgent problems that needed to be fixed at once, generating a host of vacancies to be filled quickly.

A good friend introduced me to the executive search agency De Vroedt & Thierry in Amsterdam. Given their extensive experience recruiting for senior management positions, board members and supervisory bodies they made sure to devote ample time carrying out thorough selections. This agency decided to make me a partner, and I was then lucky enough to work with a range of clients who were very serious about finding exactly the right candidates for their management teams. What stood out for me was the focus on the candidate's experience and knowledge base as well as his or her academic record and demonstrable intelligence. The process – even then – took several rounds, but in general the interviews were unfocused. The final decision on candidates was often based on the external criteria, but complemented by a healthy dose of intuition.

Intuition does have its uses, so I am not advocating that you ignore what gut instinct might tell you. There is a downside, though. Human instinct is not universally well-developed, nor is it infallible even in highly intuitive people. This book will deal with all manner of tempting traps and distractions that even experienced professionals can fall prey to. Furthermore, you would do well to be transparent about the various steps you take to make your final selections, and be able to back up your selection process with solid arguments. As a recruitment professional, you should see that an important part of your profession is to explain your selection decision and process to candidates, both those who will eventually land the jobs and those who will be passed over for specific employment positions. Both groups will benefit from this explanation.

After working in the field of executive search for a few years and having accrued some initial insights, my boyhood wonderment about success sparked my imagination again, but now with an adult focus: I began to wonder if the current methods of hiring could be improved, elevated to a higher level. My career experience aside, I decided to bring as few as possible preconceived notions or ready-made answers to my nascent quest; I would follow my itch to dig deeper. I delved into the latest research, analysed our company's methods and examined what our peers within the search-and-recruitment field were doing. Interviewing experts, successful CEOs and talented young high-potentials, I took note of what they regarded as essentials for success. In 2007, I set down what I had learned from my research in a book I called *Top Talent: the Nine Universal Criteria.** The book was well received and stimulated me to dig deeper into the subject.

Here is a quick summary of the criteria that will help you seek out, recognise and ultimately select highly talented people in various realms. They are:
- authenticity and creativity
- passion and self-motivation
- peaking at the right moment
- maintaining the ability to learn
- having the skill to reduce complexity

* *Agile Talent* is currently the only one of my books available in English.

- knowing how to set ambitious yet realistic goals
- being proactive in solving problems
- being mildly lazy or quickly bored
- possessing courage along with confidence

I realise that this list of factors for success is not perfect. However, these criteria are precisely the ones that kept cropping up in my practical experience, desk research and the interviews I conducted. They have stood the test of time. What I noticed back in 2007 was how little these success factors were related to knowledge, degrees and experience. True, these qualities are all relevant to recruitment, but they carry far less **predictive validity*** than we often assume.

Over the next few years, I extended my quest and wrote two more books – about the sense and nonsense of diversity and about leadership (*How To Become CEO,* only available in Dutch).

Three years ago, I came to realise that the world was changing much more rapidly than before, and that this pace of change would have its repercussions on the selection of talent. In the near future, the predictive validity of degrees, experience and knowledge will offer ever less viable insights into the nebulous domain that makes for candidate success. IQ will remain an important touchstone. However, brain power needs to be examined alongside the other attributes a person can bring to corporate leadership. The profound transformation of selection criteria proved to be a topic worthy of further research. It offered me ample stimulation for writing this new book, which is addressed not merely to HR managers or recruiters but to everyone involved in the management, selection and inspiration of people.

It is my hope that this book can be of value for those in top management who might fancy themselves to be above the selection process and who can just delegate the task. To do so in fact underestimates the impact of future-proof top talent in organisations.

The key themes in this book all blend seamlessly with the developments I just described. I know they will help you to answer these kinds of questions:
- How do you recruit the right people in an ever-faster-changing world in which accumulated knowledge and experience run the risk of rapidly becoming obsolete? How does the speed of technological development impact a company which depends on the agility of its employees to future-proof it?

---

* There is a glossary at the back of this book, explaining key concepts. Whenever those words appear for the first time, they are printed in bold.

- What are the criteria for selecting future-proof talent needed to reach the company's long-term targets?
- How do I shape and build the recruitment process for future-proof or agile talent, and how can I be sure that the person I select will ultimately be a perfect match for my business?
- Are there any tools or aids that can help me objectify selection methods for finding new talent? How might I shape recruitment so that bias doesn't distort the selection process?
- How do I recognise agile talent within my own organisation? And what steps can I take to improve the retention of these talented individuals?
- Are there any case studies available of businesses that seem to have found the answers to these questions, and whose experiences might benefit other organisations?
- How might I set up the selection process for future-proof talented people, in order to make our company less dependent on outside consultants?

While this book showcases an example of agile working, its main focus is not "talent within an agile working atmosphere". Instead it examines how future-proof talent seems to constantly adapt to rapid evolutions in circumstances. These developments show no signs of slowing down, nor do they leave room for slack in the constant renewal of the selection process. It would be a mistake to think the process set out in this book is etched in stone. New trends and greater insights will call for more experiments on your part, and for you to make additions to the selection process. New insights will encourage you to get rid of elements that you find have become irrelevant.

One thing is certain: the game plan in this new world is unlike anything we have ever known. It's worth repeating futurologist Alvin Toffler's insight: "The illiterate of the 21st century will not be those that cannot read or write, but those that cannot learn, unlearn and relearn."

January 2017
Ralf Knegtmans
De Vroedt & Thierry, member of Cornerstone International Group

INTRODUCTION

> ## "The information based world is moving exponentially, replacing linear thinking organisations."
>
> PETER DIAMANDIS, SINGULARITY UNIVERSITY

The world is becoming an increasingly global, digital and volatile place. As technology advances at high speed, the life cycle of business models diminishes accordingly. Nobody can miss this: anything that is mainstream today, will be outdated by tomorrow. After all, hardly more than a decade ago the world was a completely different place, as these examples from the "good old days" illustrate:

- When you wanted to buy a book, you went to a bookshop (an independent or a chain store), where the book you were after was probably out of stock, and would have to be ordered. Now, you order it from Amazon, or easier yet, download it onto your Kindle.
- If you found nothing interesting on TV during an evening, you could brave the cold weather and dash out to the video store. But chances are you wouldn't find a film that interested you. Now you watch catch-up TV or go to HBO or Netflix to binge-watch your latest must-see show. Music has gone through a similar transformation. A monthly fee to Spotify or Apple Music has replaced relatively expensive CDs, leaving you free to listen to all your favourite tunes, whenever and wherever you like, and sample the latest releases too.
- Did you ever go on holiday and just when you wanted to capture some memories on camera, you realised you had left your – recently purchased – digital camera upstairs in the hotel room? (This has happened to me more often than I care to remember.) Now, you are never without your iPhone, Samsung or other brand of smartphone, maybe complete with a selfie-stick, which lets you take fairly decent pictures. Well before you embarked on that same

holiday you would have spent several hours at a travel agent's going over the various options. Fast forward to today, and you can arrange your own travel plans – flights, rental cars, museum tickets, restaurants, and hotels – all of them sourced and booked online.

- When you wanted to share your fabulous experiences and must-see destinations with friends and family, you would call them on the overpriced hotel landline, or send them – still expensive – text messages from your mobile. Now you call on Skype (free), or send a message using WhatsApp or similar (virtually) free tools of communication. Besides, your friends will most likely have already seen your "rating" of the places you stayed at on TripAdvisor, Facebook or other social media.

Professional literature has begun to refer to today's world as the VUCA-world. This acronym stands for the four words *volatile, uncertain, complex* and *ambiguous*.

VOLATILE
UNCERTAIN
VUCA WORLD
COMPLEX
AMBIGUOUS

The pace of change not only affects humans: it also has a profound impact on companies and businesses. But whereas globally life expectancy of humans has increased by five years since 2000, on average the life cycle of companies and businesses has shortened.

This shrinking life cycle is a universal trend affecting the whole world. Claudio Feser, author of *Serial Innovators. Firms That Change the World,* notes that the average lifespan of an American business has shrunk to a mere fifteen years, compared to an average of forty-five years in the 1950s. Extrapolating from this, if businesses do not adjust their ability to innovate, their lifespan may diminish further, to no more than five to ten years in the foreseeable future. The only way to escape this fate is for businesses to compel themselves to keep on reinventing themselves.

Not only do organisations have shorter lifespans, but they also have to cope with a whole new set of foundational values. Until recently, the attempt to keep a company's knowledge concealed, or at the very least protected through patents, was nearly universal. Through the mainstreaming of the Internet, a transparent world has emerged in which sharing has become the new normal. After all, knowledge itself now has a lifespan similar to fresh fish. In fact, the speed of acquiring and using knowledge has replaced knowledge for its own sake as the key to the proverbial castle.

Along similar lines, while capital remains vital to businesses, it has ceased to be the defining factor. Neither capital nor other goods still offer any guarantee of success.

An important new business essential is the capacity to innovate. Some of the ways to do this include being aware of technological advances through, for example, the highly sophisticated automation of self-learning programmes, or the use of big data analyses to increase efficiency. Innovation can also be spurred by tapping into future-proof or **agile talent.** In brief, "agile talent" refers to professionals eager to learn and keen to innovate; they will reinvent a company from within. Before we examine this topic at length, let us enhance our understanding of disruption.

THE IMPACT OF TECHNOLOGICAL ADVANCES

The world is proving to be a place bursting at the seams through the rapid impact of technology. New market participants are often turning to unexpected business models in order to carve out significant chunks of the market for themselves. The element of surprise often gives these new entrants an unforeseen advantage. When Tesla started out in 2003, the company had never before produced a car.

"The half-life of knowledge relevance, has been diminishing and will continue to do so."

MATHIEU WEGGEMAN, AUTHOR AND PROFESSOR OF
ORGANISATION SCIENCE AND MANAGEMENT

The following chart illustrates that technological changes occur at an exponential rate, not a linear one. Linear growth happens gradually and at an equal pace, whereas exponential growth becomes ever more rapid in proportion to growing total size. This is important to remember when we are interested in nurturing the growth of companies. Nowadays exponential growth is mostly caused by the impact of computer technology on virtually every realm of business. The main reason for this can be traced to Moore's Law, which states that the power of computer chips will double every two years. At present most people still think and act in a linear manner, but if we are to succeed in the future, we will be compelled to switch from linear to exponential systems of thought. In other words, we will need to become accustomed to changes which are greater, faster and with more impact than ever before.

LINEAR GROWTH VERSUS EXPONENTIAL GROWTH

A company's turnover (its income, not staff changes) shows linear growth when annual increases are identical. Imagine starting to chart its turnover in a year in which it reaches 1 million. In the second year of linear growth turnover will increase from 1 to 2 million (1+1=2), the year after from 2 to 3 million, and so on. When we plot these numbers on a graph, they produce a straight line showing growth at a steady pace.

When a company's turnover increases at a faster than linear rate, for instance when it doubles annually, it is experiencing exponential growth. If the first year's turnover is 1 million, the second year would be 2 million, the third year would be 4 million and in the fourth year turnover would double again to 8 million. Here, the graph shows a steep upward curve instead of a gradually climbing straight line.

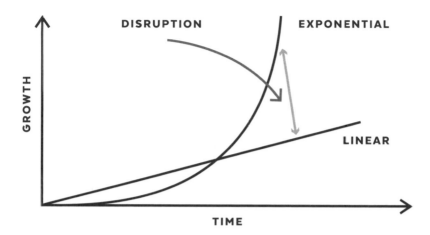

EXPONENTIAL GROWTH VERSUS LINEAR GROWTH

Other Business Models

No doubt you have heard of the following examples of new business models many times before, but their lessons are still worth examining. I refer to cutting edge businesses brought to life by digitisation. These businesses form networks and make money by matching global supply and demand 24/7, without the need for material assets or property. The world's largest taxi company owns no vehicles; the most popular media owner has no content of its own; the largest online retailer has no inventory, and the largest accommodation provider owns no real estate. Their unique selling points are something completely different.

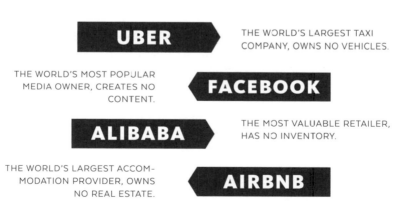

Tom Goodwin

> **"The world is changing rapidly. If we look at risk assessment in the field of small and medium-sized enterprises (SME), we always used to examine the previous three years to determine if there had been a profit. That was a reliable indicator of solvency.**
>
> **In today's context, however, this has become of negligible value, for that very same SME has to operate in a world in flux. That is why we have turned to other issues, to provide us with a higher predictive validity. An example of this might be how that entrepreneur is rated on social media."**
>
> RALPH HAMERS, CEO ING GROUP

Disruption Re-Examined

This illustration shows recent developments in business. Yet it offers no answer to the question of why the world has changed so profoundly in such a short time. All too often, the rise of startups and the appearance of so-called **disruptive innovations,** or disruption, are seen as the cause of the rapid changes in the world we live in.

There is more to this than meets the eye: while rapid technological changes cause disruption in various realms of business, this does not happen nearly as frequently as we might think. Startups have always been around as part of doing business, but have now gained in exposure compared to the past. Their ability to adapt to changes more easily than large businesses is the reason for their rise to prominence. They are no longer automatically the underdog.

Granted, disruption can have a huge impact on our new world. But I believe the term is being used far too often. Innovation is certainly not always disruptive, and research done in the United States has shown that the vast majority of startups ultimately fail. Only a small proportion of them make the transition into a scale-up. Business practices clearly show that large corporations and market leaders do in fact focus on innovation, something we will discuss in more detail in the next chapter.

But it is true that startups sometimes more or less force large businesses into changing their modus operandi. We have seen this in the finance sector, for instance.

DISRUPTION MISINTERPRETED

When most of us think of the words disruptive innovation, we recall new products and services which manage to completely overturn the familiar business model and then cause trouble for established market players. For example, WhatsApp has succeeded in pressuring the established telecom companies, and Uber is presenting a very real threat to the taxi industry. Clayton Christensen, the author of *The Innovator's Dilemma*, describes disruptive innovation as not necessarily referring to a better product for an existing target audience. He believes it is often about a simpler product, aimed at a target audience overlooked by current market players. This audience – the budget end of the market made up of consumers with little spending power and low expectations – are usually deemed to be of marginal relevance. Initially, the existing market players do not feel threatened by the new products or services. After all, perched at the top of the market, they can look down on marginal clients. At first they hardly appreciate these stealth products – even thinking they are inferior – though they are in fact highly valued and purchased by the outlier audience.

The new entries on the market then go on to improve their products and services, catering to the lowest point of the market. These refinements lead to higher quality and the next thing you know, the mid-price market share opens up. By the time the established businesses catch on, it is often too late to stop the new entries eating into "their" market. Clayton Christensen clarifies the nature of a specific type of startup through his description of disruption. Initially, these startups tend to focus on an apparently insignificant market share. This strategy sets them apart from startups which aim straight at the core of the established businesses' market share. Often buoyed up by immediate response, they are ultimately acquired before they can present any serious kind of threat.

Even when disruptive innovation is not the cause of the decline in business lifespan, the fact remains that this life cycle has shortened significantly as a result of technological changes. Organisations then need to keep reinventing themselves if they want to try and turn the tide. Tesla, Uber and Airbnb are among these relatively new businesses which pop up out of nowhere, go on to claim large chunks of the market and prove that even highly reputable companies are not invincible.

"Uber became a serious business over the course of three years. At the same rate, an established company can crumble and disintegrate. Just remember Nokia, formerly a decisively cutting-edge business. A CEO no longer has the luxury to waste away years blindly muddling along. When you come to think of it like that, a proper assessment of the quality of leadership and management is more crucial than ever."

FRANS VAN HOUTEN, CEO ROYAL PHILIPS

From Hero to Zero: Nokia & Kodak

The recent experiences of Nokia and Kodak only help to show us the full extent of these developments.

Despite its history of reinvention, transforming itself from a wood pulp plant to a producer of rubber items to PCs and mobile phones, Nokia ultimately failed to take decisive action in newly changed circumstances. A solid market leader for years, leaving its competition in the dust, the Finnish phone producer had record sales in 2007, but then found itself on the brink of disaster through lack of innovation. Way back when, the ever-present and indestructible models Nokia 3210 and 3310 could be found in the backpacks and jeans pockets of students and school children all over the world. Still, the global success of the business was to come to a crashing halt. As the world was going through tumultuous change, the Finnish board of directors may have been saying they wanted to innovate, though they failed to implement said innovation. Case in point, they waited too long to adopt the operating system Symbian. This failure allowed Google and Apple to zoom past the formerly savvy Fins. Ultimately, Microsoft ended up acquiring the telephone company and Nokia's history of change proved immaterial. It all came down to a single instance of innovating too little, too late. Not overnight, but in just a few years' time, a well-known brand ended up at a dead end.

Kodak has a similar tale to tell. This renowned photographic brand was a key player in its field, exerting a huge impact on the market. When a brand has conquered the market to the extent that people call taking a snapshot "a Kodak moment", you assume they are here to stay. In fact, it was not the disruptive innovation which would push the giant of photography and film to the edge. Kodak had been one of the first companies to adopt digital photography and held many patents in this new field. Sadly, the company lacked the ability to adapt to a world in flux, its leadership failing to properly move the organisation into the digital age through its company procedures. Kodak ended up in the same sad spot as Nokia.

Two highly esteemed brands were stripped of their standing and market position, thanks to their incapacity to innovate.

AGILITY

You might be thinking, as I did at first, that the pace of technological and other changes will not be as pervasive as it seems. You might be thinking that while popular brands like Netflix, Google, PayPal and Spotify are the ones who are at the forefront of all this change, the ones who have adopted agility at work, in the everyday world large and small businesses will end up muddling through as before. Let me suggest you watch the video *Humans Need Not Apply* by C.C.P. Grey.* This short film provides a clear and concise look at how digitisation, robotisation and the speed of change are having a huge impact on business across the board. After watching it, you will probably agree with me that there are only two sure things in our world in flux: rapid change and uncertainty. In the future strategic adaptability has to be the top priority. Agility will be the number one prerequisite.

"Agility" as I see it can best be defined as fast, pliable and in constant motion. It is comprised of two key components that interact positively:

1. First of all, it refers to the nimbleness and astuteness with which an organisation proactively acts on market opportunities.

2. Secondly, it makes reference to the resilience of an organisation in coping with the increased volatility of the market and the massive, unforeseen changes the world is facing.

AGILE TALENT

My definition of agile talent focuses on those talented people who possess the ability to adapt quickly and efficiently to changing backgrounds or circumstances. If we add this idea to the previously described two components of agility, we will see a multi-faceted concept emerge. People who possess agile talent are keen to and able to discern patterns in their experiences; they possess a rich capacity for learning. This capacity encompasses the ability to *unlearn* old tricks and habits. Agile talent is

* *Humans Need Not Apply* on YouTube: https://youtu.be/7Pq-S557XQU.

resilient, adaptable and excels at translating what it has learnt into new methods and actions. Being able to implement any new knowledge is an absolute given.

Whereas you might be familiar with the developments described so far, not all of us are acting upon what we know here. Common sense is not always common practice. Broadly speaking, the reason for this is that it is easier to talk about rather than implement these insights. Familiar ways of working and old habits die hard.

However, if businesses want to legitimise their *raison d'être,* they need to be willing and able to renew and reinvent themselves all the time. Adaptability and a willingness to change will be of crucial importance. They can drive that change by implementing procedures that foster innovation and creating an innovation-friendly company culture, an environment where there is room for experimenting and mistakes. After all, there is no truer path to learning than by making mistakes.

Innovation does not mean having to completely reinvent the wheel on your own. Turning your attention to impressive examples from other realms or sectors of business than your own can be both valuable and inspiring.

Where can you find such examples?

Nature's Adaptability

Oddly enough, nature offers us the very best example of innovation and smart adaptability, as Ylva Poelman, an expert on innovation, explains in her book *Nature's Invention.* The book has a simple message: for close to four billion years nature has deployed an unparalleled system of intelligent and efficient innovation using natural selection as a guiding principle. As a result of this innovative ability, organisms are capable of adapting, and nature never stops existing in spite of changing circumstances – exploding volcanoes, ice ages, massive fires, hurricanes or invasive species. Through all the disruptions in the environment organisms never stop changing; the only constant is that everything changes.

* Currently only available in Dutch.

Ylva Poelman lists many examples of how nature has inspired human innovation, including:

- Pain-free needles for injections, inspired by a specific type of mosquito.
- Optimisation algorithms applied to – for example – internet traffic.
- A high-speed train with an aerodynamically shaped nose inspired by a kingfisher.
- Highly sensitive sensors based on the senses of insects.
- Dirt-repellent paints and coatings, based on the self-cleaning leaves of the lotus plant.
- Aircraft and ship efficiencies based on characteristics of shark skin.

The common denominator of these examples is that natural technology nearly always outdoes our human technology. Insects have senses that are many times more sophisticated and efficient than sensors designed and used by us. Similarly, ants, bees and other simple organisms are extremely efficient at finding the quickest route or coming up with the best division of labour. Nature certainly has much to inspire us whenever we want to get serious about innovation. **Optimisation algorithms** which were inspired by nature may underperform slightly, in predictable situations, but they never fail to deliver in unpredictable and varied situations.*

Recalling Darwin's maxim, we might say that it is no longer the greatest or strongest who will survive, but those who are best suited to adapt swiftly to new situations. This aphorism applies to businesses as well: their only real chance of survival is to be agile in a world in flux. And drilling down we find that agile companies owe most of their success to resilient and agile talent. In this book I would like to share my ideas on how to recognise and recruit this kind of talent, ideas which have been shaped through research and many interviews with CEOs, HR managers and other experts in the field. Here you will find how to recognise and recruit these talented individuals who will work with you to make your organisation future-proof and agile.

* Ylva Poelman (September 2, 2015). "Van de servers en de bijtjes." *Trouw*.

FURTHER READING

BOOKS

- Erik Brynjolfsson & Andrew McAfee (2014). *The Second Machine Age. Work, Progress, and Prosperity in a Time of Brilliant Technologies.* W.W. Norton.
- Clayton M. Christensen (1997). *The Innovator's Dilemma. When New Technologies Cause Great Firms to Fail.* Harvard Business Review Press.
- Claudio Feser (2011). *Serial Innovators. Firms That Change the World.* Wiley.
- Lynda Gratton (2011). *The Shift. The Future of Work Is Already Here.* Collins.
- Salim Ismail, Michael S. Malone & Yuri van Geest (2014). *Exponential Organizations.* Diversion Books.

ARTICLES

- Clayton M. Christensen, Michael E. Raynor & Rory McDonald (December 2015). "What Is Disruptive Innovation?" *Harvard Business Review.*

PART 1. RAPID DEVELOPMENTS AND SELECTIONS THAT FAIL

"In the future, when selecting agile talent your focus needs to shift from discerning the skills someone already has to recognising the ability to understand and solve the dilemmas of tomorrow, of next week and of next year."

In this section of the book, we will turn our attention to how global developments impact organisations. Going beyond the way startups respond to changes, we will look at the capacity for change at large corporate organisations. What can we learn from case studies involving such organisations? How did they structure their organisation, and how do they select talent that will provide a longer proverbial shelf life? What developments can we expect in the job market and how will these advances influence the criteria we apply when we select talent?

CAPACITY FOR CHANGE IN OIL TANKERS

"Failure isn't fatal, but failure to change might be."

JOHN WOODEN, COACH

My curiosity was piqued by the short film *Humans Need Not Apply,* mentioned in the previous chapter. I felt the need to delve deeper into its subject matter. To what extent did the developments in this clip capture the corporate world? Startups and tech companies were at the heart of my research into the speed of technological changes and the new criteria for agile talent. I was particularly keen to find out how willing to change larger companies were, especially ones with longer and more traditional backgrounds. I was interested in meeting with several relatively new CEOs and COOs of organisations like these, to learn what their views on this topic would be. Royal Philips came to mind instantly, on account of it being very much an organisation in flux, with CEO Frans van Houten having been appointed in 2011, in the wake of the financial crisis. This was a time during which many companies were forced to take a close look at their business models and rethink them accordingly.

NEW DIRECTIONS FOR PHILIPS

When Frans van Houten and I sat down to talk, the company was thoroughly rethinking its strategy. He had a clear grasp of the situation: the rapid global developments called for a corporate change of direction. In our interview, he described how the light bulb factory of days gone by had undergone a complete transformation of its mission – even, you might say, of its essence.

"We have noticed that as far as Philips is concerned, a business model founded purely on products has become obsolete. First of all, because innovation is based on the whole system, not on one single product. To give an example, you could give away free hardware, when your profits are based on the services which surround the product in question, such as big data and advertising. Several years ago, we realised that the old and familiar business model which had led Philips to greatness – i.e. sales of standardised products – had in fact become outdated, particularly where B2B was concerned. We need to transform ourselves from product-based to system-based (through integration), and reshape ourselves from a company focused on production, to one that is customer-oriented. For instance, we now provide ten-year contracts for hospitals, in which we completely take over their technology and all its attendant problems. This is a radically different business model, requiring different talent and a completely altered mindset. A move from short-term thinking, to long-term thinking. From working in separate silos to collaborating, and so on."

Apart from Royal Philips, I wanted to review an organisation from a sector which most people regard as fairly conservative and unwilling to change. A business acquaintance suggested ING to me after he heard about them fundamentally rethinking the strategy of part of the Dutch business unit. After ING The Netherlands launched its new strategy in 2015, I decided to start my research there. It would end up providing valuable information on the recent transformation which part of this multinational had gone through. The reason why I was so interested in ING The Netherlands, is that it is one of the very few large businesses in the Netherlands which has adopted agile working – in a significant part of the Dutch organisation, at least. ING The Netherlands illustrates vividly the issues involved in agile working. If you are already familiar with agile working, this will be a familiar scene for you. In that case, allow me to steer you towards the chapter on "Employagility" on page 40.

Hoping to learn all about the various transformations, I sat down with CEO Ralph Hamers, COO The Netherlands Bart Schlatmann, and Maarten van Beek, HR Director for the Netherlands.

VISION IN MANAGEMENT

Even though ING The Netherlands had not been burnt too badly in the crisis and the general feeling was that they had emerged stronger, management at the top of the company was adamant that the organisation should not rest on its laurels. They simply could not afford to, not in today's world. They saw the world in flux, with Internet and technology having more impact every single day. A few years ago, no one would have dreamed that Facebook and Apple would offer their users payment facilities. Still, ING management was convinced that change was in the wind – a change which would have a profound effect on banking and the way people worked in this field.

"Information is being shared more quickly, thanks to the growing impact of the Internet. New entrants to the market are able to reach large chunks of potential customers through this impact, too. Market boundaries are starting to blur, with markets no longer exclusively being accessed from within a particular field, and with technological possibilities being copied more often and more easily than ever. Besides, consumers are more vocal, more demanding and less loyal to brands than they used to be. Anyone wanting to keep their customers happy and leave the competition behind needs to be fast and agile, too," is how Ralph Hamers sums up the vision of ING management.

The Impact of FinTechs

Hamers and his team noticed a second development – one that complemented their desire to lionise the customer and better respond to client needs swiftly and adequately – which they were certain would alter the field of finance for many years to come: FinTechs.

> **"More than 20% of financial service business is at risk to FinTechs by 2020. And consumer banking and payments will be the most exposed in the near future."**
>
> PWC, *GLOBAL FINTECH REPORT 2016*

FinTech is shorthand for the words "financial" and "technology". Businesses involved in FinTech are usually small and flexible. Their focus is the niche market within a certain field. "FinTech" has come to refer to businesses affecting lasting change in the financial world through innovative products and services. Any FinTech initiative has the full range of financial service as its playground. Pay facilities, corporate credit lines or corporate credit approval are a few examples. A global report by PwC published in 2016 points out how these FinTech organisations will radically redefine the realm of finance. In the future, a bank will simply be a value aggregator. In layman's terms, this means that some applications or functions will be designed in-house, but they will be supplemented by outside parties, providing software, for instance. The main goal is to offer the best possible service platform to one's customers. Banking is not the only field where this development is playing out. Just think of Uber, the taxi company. This company develops some of its software, but complements its in-house technology with products from a host of other companies.

Joining Hands

Though many other organisations have opted for a wait-and-see approach, expecting it all to blow over, the new chairman at ING and his team were determined to take a proactive approach. They would be the change they wished to see in the world. FinTechs inspired them to look for opportunities to collaborate with other firms rather than to dig themselves into a trench and bitterly defend their position. I would not be surprised if Hamers and his senior managers had heard of the well-known aphorism, "Offence is the best defence."

The board of ING now faced the daunting task of moving from a new vision to a cultural shift within the company. Creating a way to help the company cultivate adaptability and responsiveness to change in its very core was the next step.

"The question before us is what the bank of the future ought to focus on. Our answer is that we have committed ourselves to providing a differentiated customer experience. That, in a nutshell, is our main focus. Our first priority is: how can we remain relevant in customer service?

That may mean that one of our own products stays on the books, or that another party's product may end up on their own books. We will have to take this decision as it comes. When we were devising our strategy, we consciously asked ourselves: do we want to be the railway tracks, or the train riding along them? The tracks are the books and the train is the customer experience. We never had any doubts, being the latter was the obvious choice."

RALPH HAMERS, CEO ING GROUP

Introspection and Learning from Others

ING came up with a new strategy which they named RIO. This acronym stands for Redesign Into Omnichannel. For ING, this is a decisive statement that banks are actually tech companies, resembling the likes of Google, Amazon or Airbnb. Through introspection and the examination of the outside world – a feat I will return to later in the book – ING even looked beyond their own business sector and examined how companies operating in sectors alien to the banking experts were excelling at rapid adaptability in a world in flux. RIO would later adopt the motto, "Empowering people to stay a step ahead in life and business."

Agile Manifesto

First of all, ING analysed how these businesses were organised according to their corporate values. Next, they looked at how they had set up and implemented agile working. Virtually all of the organisations that were examined used the principles of the so-called *agile manifesto.** It is a manifesto consisting of twelve rules that are to be implemented all at once. Agile businesses stand out from more traditional organisations by their ability to respond instantly to changing customer demands and market situations. One characteristic that stood out was the speed at which they managed to introduce new customer functionalities. The essentials of this manifesto include:

- Customer satisfaction, which is to be achieved through outstanding performance.
- Limited hierarchy.
- Informal company culture, aimed at easy cooperation, communication and focus on a common goal. (The interests of the team are more important than the individual's, so massive egos need not apply.)
- Small and multifunctional teams with business managers and IT staffers on the same team – everyone works together closely.
- Decisions are based on thorough analyses of the data. In other words, everything is measured – people do not merely work according to their instincts.
- Short and ongoing cycles of small improvements. For these, ING has coined the phrase **Minimum Viable Products (MVPs)**. Based on customer feedback, MVPs are constantly tweaked.
- Simplicity first! Simplicity is vital. Reducing complexity takes precedence over making things more complicated.

While this manifesto may be focused mainly on software development, it does in fact provide valuable tools for agile working everywhere.

Doing Implementation by Halves: A Bad Idea

After examining how other companies had adapted their organisation to agile working, ING turned their attention to the bottlenecks in the current working methods identified by managers and staffers alike. One of the main weaknesses which surfaced during this internal analysis was the preference

* An example of such a manifesto can be found at www.agilemanifesto.org.

for working in **silos,** instead of actively cooperating across a range of different departments. Another was the top-down hierarchy of responsibility, instead of deploying an agile model in which multifunctional teams are in charge of the whole decision chain.

The principles of agile working were not completely new to ING at that time – this way of working had been implemented in several parts of the organisation – but somehow it was never fully implemented throughout the company. The manifesto requires it be fully implemented, with no exceptions. "If your aim is to turn your organisation into one that is agile in its operation, it is crucial to be consistent in the application of the agile manifesto, to cohesively adhere to its principles, and to create end-to-end responsibility," explains Bart Schlatmann, the COO for the Netherlands who was responsible for the changes at the time. "That is often what goes wrong within companies. They manage to transform one or more business units, but fail to extend the changes to the whole chain or organisation."

"If you are truly determined to adopt a new and agile way of working, the bottom line is: how much are you willing to surrender? If you are not willing to apply all the principles of the agile manifesto and delegate end-to-end responsibility to multifunctional teams, which oversee the whole chain, then you are heading for failure."

BART SCHLATMANN, COO ING THE NETHERLANDS

ING drew up this concise overview of the targets for the new working style:
- A vastly increased focus on the customer.
- Shorter time to market: a noticeable reduction in the development time for new products and services, in order to be more responsive in addressing significant changes in customer demands.
- Fewer obstacles for teams and individuals, thus improving their room to manoeuver and work together and empowering them in the process.

- More highly motivated and passionate staff members, employees who have "self-starter" as their middle name

ING now accomplishes more with fewer people, which leads to cost reduction and higher profits. The lower costs are an added boon, not a goal of the transformation. Creating the best possible service level and cutting down the time needed to adopt improvements in customer service were higher on the list than reducing costs.

Agile Organisation

In general, agile businesses tend to organise work around small, multidisciplinary and self-steering teams, often named **squads**. They consist of no more than nine staff members. Each squad works toward its own team goal. In this kind of structure the traditional department has become a relic. Also banished is the "creative graveyard" syndrome, in which a significant innovation developed by one department is not even looked at, let alone considered for implementation by the next silo in the hierarchy. It gets consigned to the graveyard of promising advances.

The separate multidisciplinary teams or squads are fully responsible (that is, they have end-to-end responsibility) for the development and implementation of all customer missions or challenges. These client targets might consist of an entirely new product or service, or some part of it, such as reaching optimal customer satisfaction and shortening the process of mortgage applications at the same time. ING put this approach into practice by flattening the organisational hierarchy: the board set specific goals, which were then adopted by the **tribes**. A tribe is a collection of squads working in one particular field, with its own relevant goals. One such goal might be the creation of something called a "WOW" at ING. WOW is an acronym standing for We Outperform (your) Wishes, and is an immediate result of aiming for an improved degree of customer focus. Broadly speaking, agile companies set themselves a particular "higher" purpose. As a rule, a purpose will refer to a highly ambitious and ground-breaking goal, which need not have any connection to the product or services at hand.

More on Squads

Squads are small groups of staff members from a variety of backgrounds, for example IT experts, product or brand managers, marketers and data analysts. They join forces around a specific idea or a target which needs to be swiftly moved along to the first stage of testing. The best way to describe how they work is to focus on their ongoing team performance and the results they produce. Squads at ING are obligated to deliver a new customer functionality every three weeks. They must also measure the results of these innovations. The endless meetings of the old days have been replaced by working in short data-driven bursts or cycles, with ongoing testing of products and the quick adaptation of successful innovations. A key characteristic of the squad process is frequent but targeted communication – no formula-mandated meetings.

"The traditional organisation with its hierarchy, with ample room for tepid bureaucracy, have been replaced by a more simple and flexible organisation. Here, the team goals always overrule the individual ones."

MAARTEN VAN BEEK, HR DIRECTOR ING THE NETHERLANDS

Communication takes place within teams, between teams, and laterally between individuals of different teams. The high degree of squad autonomy may suggest otherwise, but they are in fact meant to contribute to the overall company goals. Squads do not have traditional managers; instead several tasks are divided among three separate roles: product owner, chapter lead and agile coach. They each play a part in realising the mission of the squad.

ROLES WITHIN A SQUAD

Besides overseeing the everyday tasks of each squad member, the product owner is responsible for monitoring the squad's backlog and adjusting tasks where needed. In agile working, a backlog is best described as a to-do list of items which require attention ranked according to the priorities the product owner determines. Once a week, the product owner, the chapter lead and the agile coaches sit down to draw up a progress report, or assessment of what is called "velocity". The team's performance is discussed too. The chapter lead and agile coaches then transfer any input from this meeting into their own work.

The chapter lead is a leader who has a hands-on role within the squad. (This way of working has no room for traditional management positions.) Seven squad members report to the chapter lead. In fact, the chapter lead will be responsible for a particular field of expertise, such as relevant legislation and regulations, or some specific type of knowledge within IT, on top of their everyday work as a squad member. Keeping that field of expertise up-to-date and sharing this knowledge with the rest of the tribe are essential. In turn, the chapter lead reports to the tribe lead.

The agile coaches are responsible for creating excellent teams. Even when a team is performing well, the coaches never stop looking for ways to improve performance. In a sense, you could compare them to a football coach. They share the responsibility for a squad's results, even though they do not do any programming themselves. After liaising with the product owner and the chapter lead, they set out to assemble the perfect team for a particular squad purpose. They play a key role in promoting the new company culture and take great care to prevent people from reverting to old habits. As such, they are crucial to the success of the transformation from old working methods to new ones. The agile coaches will remain as a cornerstone of the company's ongoing commitment to the new style of working.

The new way of working leaves little room for hierarchy. The traditional organisation with its hierarchy and tepid bureaucracy has been replaced by a more simple and flexible organisation. Here, the team goals always overrule the individual ones.

COMPOSITION OF A SQUAD

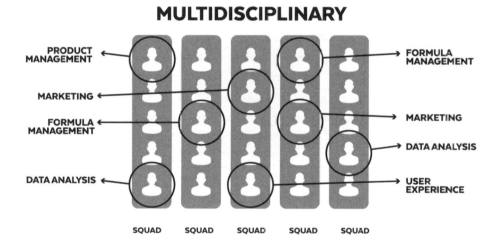

SQUADS ARE MULTIDISCIPLINARY

Tribes

With the workforce divided into autonomous squads the question of fitting these squads into an integrated corporate structure becomes important. After all, they are meant to operate independently and steer themselves. This is where the tribes come into play. All the squads with similar goals make up a co-ordinating whole, a.k.a. the tribe, which has its own mission. For example, ING tribes include the mortgage services tribe, the investments & private banking tribe, and the experience omnichannel tribe. The operating rule is that the different squads need to confer with each other regularly if they are to work together effectively.

Following Malcolm Gladwell's "Rule of 150",* ING's tribes consist of no more than 150 people. ING found that this number did indeed encourage impromptu interactions between squads.

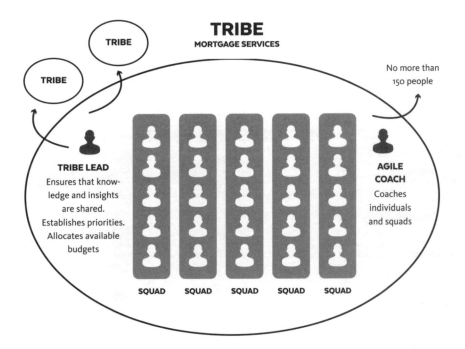

EXAMPLE OF A TRIBE

Flexible and Custom-Made Service

The great advantage of this agile way of working is that it enables ING, a large multinational, to respond swiftly and flexibly to changing events – and to its clients. For example, a new and free app enables customers to offer real-time comments on the service or interaction they have had with an ING staff member. By putting a tick mark on a smiley face in green, red or an in-between colour, customers can indicate immediately and personally how they felt about

---

* In his book *The Tipping Point* (Little, Brown, 2001) Gladwell cites Dunbar's number, which states that people can maintain social relationships with no more than 150 people; beyond this number working with and relating to others becomes difficult.

the service. The bank is then able to respond to this feedback directly. Today's customer is looking for a quick and personal client experience, and ING's surveys and bottom line results reinforce their conviction that this approach produces increasingly loyal customers. The Zappos model, an American on-line shoe retailer innovation, inspired ING to restructure their traditional call centre into a cutting-edge service. Now, the ING staffer taking a call is able to provide end-to-end customer service; no longer does the customer get caught up in a referral run-around. ING staff members are given a great deal of free-dom to make decisions on how to best serve the customer or even exceed ex-pectations (WOW – We Outperform your Wishes). This is another example of ING absorbing valuable lessons from businesses in very different realms.

Constantly Evaluating and Adapting

A key characteristic of the new way of working exemplified by ING is its con-stant evolution. New models and working styles may be examined and even implemented, but none of them are etched in stone. Everything is measured, examined critically, and adjusted accordingly. Just because something might work perfectly today is no guarantee it will satisfy tomorrow's needs. The main corporate driver is to stay ahead of the constant stream of rapid changes and provide the customer with the best, fastest, most relevant and most personal level of service possible.

ING introduced their employees and suppliers to their "New Way of Work-ing" in a video of that name produced just before the major changes to an agile structure were implemented.* While it can come across as rather academic, it paints a clear picture of the new organisational structure and the ways in which people work together.

Agile Selection

At the same time as implementing agile working, ING altered its system for se-lecting new employees – a process that I was particularly interested in. It's all very well to restructure your organisation along agile lines, but to successfully "walk the talk" requires a different type of employee.

The old-school method of talent selection called for a manager within the hierarchy to be responsible for hiring new people. The new method aimed at

---

* The film is available on YouTube: *Agile Way of Working at ING Netherlands*.
  https://www.youtube.com/watch?v=NcBoZKWAPAo

finding agile talent entrusts a committee of peers to make selections. In addition to peer selection, ING makes a conscious effort to base selections on a prospective employee's personality and cultural identity, not just on skills and experience. Is this candidate a good match with the company culture, is his or her personality in sync with agile working? How well does his or her primary social motive match the organisation's? Apart from the interview focused on questions of this nature, other tools are used in this selection process, including 360-degree-feedback and specific testing methodology. For the tribe lead position, these tests might include the Big Five personality test or the TAT-test, which looks at motivational needs. Finally, an applicant's personal objectives will be compared to ING's corporate purpose.

Peer Selection in Action

The new selection process involves interviews conducted in pairs according to the "four eyes-principle". This is something I will discuss at length in step 3. Different duos of alternating members of staff will interview a candidate for a specific position. This means a candidate will be assessed by very different people, from alternating perspectives. After these interviews, there is a calibration or evaluation of the candidate. An essential feature of this process is that the final assessment of a candidate is never based on one single assessment. Instead candidates pass through a range of interviews and selection tools. To maintain objectivity, it is vitally important that the interviewers do not share their findings and results during the selection process. All the impressions, findings and test results are brought together in the calibration.

This method of selecting people provides a better and more objective view of candidates, filtering out anomalous choices and highlighting more subtle distinctions. In a formal sense the "receiving" manager, who the new hire will report to, does have veto power, provided he can argue why he cannot or will not work with the candidate. In practice this veto is rarely exercised. After all, it would be foolhardy to callously discard an assessment that has been thoroughly evaluated by a full committee of selecting peers.

Practise What You Preach

When I visited ING headquarters, it was immediately obvious that the place had retired its former stolid financial service structure. I beheld large open spaces bedecked with long tables, beanbag chairs along with stylish chairs and sofas, wall coverings made of moss, and lots of inviting work areas. The whole look reminded me more of a hi-tech company than the pinstriped behemoth of yesteryear. Nearly all the glass conference rooms are named after business leaders famous for agile business practices, such as Steve Jobs, Mark Zuckerberg and Richard Branson. Strolling further inside, you cannot miss the huge whiteboards festooned with bright ideas. Walls are adorned with Post-its, some of them filled with detailed plans, others with just a word or two scrawled on them. At the far end of the corridor, I catch a glimpse of an airy and modern staff cafeteria. There is a hint of chaos about the place, as people sit huddled in teams, discussing their work, and others stand around chatting. A games room with pool table and air hockey paraphernalia hint at the happy blend of work and play. The whole place is absolutely teeming with activity. You cannot possibly be mistaken: "creativity rules" here.

"A certain degree of trial and error will determine what works and what does not. There is no permanent and final organisational structure. While the business model contains certain building blocks, like the tribes and squads, it keeps evolving as well. In a nutshell, the agile approach needs to display agility itself."

NICK JUE, CEO ING THE NETHERLANDS

Resistance?

I had a chance to talk to employees; in addition to many upbeat stories about this work arrangement they shared with me, there were of course people who openly expressed their doubts about all the new-fangled ideas and their workability. Some of the critics are now working for competitors, some are now former associates and others are people still involved in the company.

Bart Schlatmann is singularly unmoved by the naysayers. The main reason is that the new way of working has truly taken hold, most notably in an increased commitment to customer service. ING made a practice of visiting cutting edge businesses like Spotify in the early days of their new business model, and now they often show visiting tech companies around ING. The "techies" are keen to learn from them. While Schlatmann is gratified by the attention ING has garnered in the business community, he is convinced that ING is not riding on the fad of the day. He is certain that the agile approach addresses the specific needs of today's business world. At the same time assembling the workforce into squads by nature addresses specific targets and circumstances. Each target raises the issue: is a squad the right way to go in this instance? There are parts of the organisation where the answer may be "no". In the future, trial and error will decide.

There is no permanent and final organisational structure. The agile approach needs to show agility itself – it cannot by definition be etched in stone, nor is it a goal for its own sake.

"EMPLOYAGILITY"

The new work models at ING The Netherlands hold useful pointers for other businesses wanting to improve their own agility. It is essential at the outset that businesses keep in mind that this is a fundamentally different way to work. There is less hierarchy, less control and fewer levels of management. On the other hand there are more questions, fewer strict plans, more experiments in "short bursts" and more adaptations in the way that people work. This in turn impacts on how staff is selected, and of course on the talent already working for you.

From now on employees at all levels will have to deal with a job market in flux – including at their present place of employment. Additionally, they will have to be prepared to learn and implement entirely new skills. No one will be able to escape the consequences. Those thinking that the impact of robotics, 3D-printing and artificial intelligence will be confined to unskilled work are mistaken. To return once again to the video *Humans Need Not Apply*, professionals (notaries, doctors, lawyers, and the like) and those engaged in creative occupations will feel the impact as well. No one will remain immune.

For talented individuals, this means they will see jobs and positions mutate in the very near future. It will not be long before young notary publics or lawyers will see their profession altered beyond recognition. Jobs will not only mutate – MIT professors Erik Brynjolfsson and Andrew McAfee predict that a huge proportion of jobs will disappear altogether over the next few decades. Their pessimistic outlook is echoed by Oxford University's Carl Benedikt Frey and Michael Osborne whose research suggests that roughly 47 percent of American jobs are at risk of being computerised and disappearing.

These studies clearly show that every single employee needs to be committed to ongoing training, development and education, sometimes even going so far as to retrain for a whole new career. Lifelong learning is no longer a luxury. It has become a prerequisite for us all.

From the employer perspective, these gloomy predictions point to an extra dimension of business agility: clearly, the degree of agility driving an organisation is determined largely by the agility of its employees. There is a mutually beneficial need for employees and organisations to respond promptly to changes and contribute to the value chain. PwC names this "employagility".[*]

"47 percent of total US employment is at risk to be automated over the next decade or two."

CARL BENEDIKT FREY AND MICHAEL A OSBORNE, OXFORD UNIVERSITY

OTHER SKILLS

To keep one's appeal to employers while competing with "self-learning" robots and computers, the employee of the future simply must be agile. Amongst other things, this means excelling at those characteristics which are as yet out of bounds for computers. Intuition is one capacity that comes to mind. The ability to analyse and interpret data, to be a good judge of character, to be endowed with compassion and creativity are a few more.

[*] PwC (December 2015). *Digitalisering en robotisering vragen om employagility. De toekomst van de arbeidsmarkt in de zakelijke en financiële dienstverlening.* PwC.

CONCLUSION

Over the last couple of decades, IQ, skills and experience have been key employee selection factors. These criteria remain valid, but others will gain traction and might even become decisive as businesses rethink their selection procedures. The employee of the future shall have to possess a radically different skill set. In turn, this implies a new selection strategy. This idea is at the very heart of this book. (But note that this book does not cover the recruitment of staff – by which I mean methods of advertising for and finding prospective employees. This is an interesting topic in itself, but is another subject.)

How can we improve the way in which we select staff? How might we achieve a smarter way of selecting if the past experience of prospective employees cannot offer any future guarantees? Which characteristics of talent are the bare minimum for you to take into account in your selection process? How reliable are your criteria? In the following pages of this book I will share with you my lessons and insights drawn from the past 17 years in talent selection, supplemented with the opinions of other experts in talent management and assessment as well as today's leading thinkers and agile talents. Allow me to recommend that you immerse yourself in the theory on motivational needs and personality. Next, experiment with the tried and tested method presented in this book. You will soon notice a significant improvement in your predictions of future success of your candidates. An added benefit is that you will no longer experience the need to appeal to outside consultants for your selection of future-proof and agile talent.

We will begin by touching upon theories of motivational needs and personality. Then I will disclose a method of talent selection consisting of three stages divided into nine steps which my colleagues and I apply every day. Putting this method into practice will deliver significant improvements in your ability to select successful candidates.

FURTHER READING

BOOKS

- Tony Hsieh (2010). *Delivering Happiness. A Path to Profits, Passion, and Purpose.* Grand Central Publishing.
- Eric Ries (2011). *The Lean Startup. How Relentless Change Creates Radically Succesful Businesses.* Penguin Books Ltd.
- Marcus Ries & Diana Summers (2016). *Agile Project Management. A Complete Beginner's Guide To Agile Project Management.* CreateSpace Independent Publishing Platform.
- Chris Sims & Hillary Louise Johnson (2011). *The Elements of Scrum.* Dymaxicon.
- Jeff Sutherland (2014). *Scrum. A Revolutionary Approach to Building Teams, Beating Deadlines and Boosting Productivity.* RH Business Books.

ARTICLES

- Carl Benedikt Frey & Michael A. Osborne (September 17, 2013). *The Future of Employment. How Susceptible Are Jobs to Computerisation?* Working paper. University of Oxford.
- Mark Hulshof (Oktober 1, 2014). "Strategic Agility: The All-Important Process." LinkedIn. Excerpt from: Mark Hulshof, Sjors van Leeuwen & Jesse Meijers (2013). *Strategic agility.* Triggre B.V.
- PwC (March 2016). *Global FinTech Report. Blurred Lines: How FinTech Is Shaping Financial Services.* PwC.

ANALYSIS: WHEN SELECTION MISSES ITS MARK

"What we need is more people who specialise in the impossible."

THEODORE ROETHKE, AMERICAN POET

Our previous chapter dealt with the relevance of agile talent. This chapter will deal with today's practice of selecting talent, often a hit-and-miss procedure. Where do things go wrong? How might you prevent hiring mistakes from happening? In this section of the book, I will examine the tendency to limit selection criteria to IQ, skills and experience. Next, I will discuss two other common issues: mismatching the job criteria to the specific context of the company, and interviewing candidates using highly unstructured methods.

Too frequently, people limit the tools they use in the selection process, which is not at all a smart move. It is a well-researched fact that combining various tests and techniques in the course of the selection produces significantly improved predictions of candidates' future success. There are of course many other examples of mistakes in this field, but I firmly believe that these are the most significant ones.

PENNY WISE, POUND FOOLISH?

Selecting the right person for the job is hard. It is an important, yet complicated part of what managers do. To my knowledge, almost all organisations take the selection of talent seriously. Still, the practice of everyday selection is rife with mistakes. Nowadays, any organisation worth its salt has a professional human resources department. They train their recruiters and management, and they spend a lot of money bringing in outside consultants. In spite of all this, the SHRM Foundation* reports that a stunning 50 percent of newly acquired top management positions fail within the first eighteen months. Two key reasons for this failure are the absence of an assessment of risks or **derailers** and the fact that the company has not set up a satisfactory **onboarding** programme, with an emphasis on effective learning.

The Chartered Institute of Personnel and Development (CIPD) has calculated that a management mismatch costs roughly 2.5 times what that person makes in a year. Harvard Business School has produced research showing that this figure is even higher, up to 3-to-5 times the annual salary, and possibly ten times in the case of highly specialist positions or top executives. The figures for a CEO or chairman of the board are undoubtedly higher.

In other words, it makes sense to keep mistakes within recruitment and selection of new talent to an absolute minimum, if only for reasons of cost-effectiveness.

"According to the CIPD, a candidate mismatch costs roughly 2.5 times what that person makes in a year. Harvard Business School has produced research showing that this figure is even higher, up to 3-to-5 times what the annual salary is, and possibly ten times in the case of highly specialist positions or general top executives."

FROM: EFINANCIALCAREERS, FEBRUARY 2012

---

* Talya N. Bauer (2010). *Onboarding New Employees: Maximizing Success.* SHRM Foundation.

RECRUITMENT NOT LIMITED TO RECRUITERS

In today's world, nearly every organisation will assure you that people are their most valuable asset. These fine words do not necessarily mean that the company pays proper respect and attention to that asset, though. Whenever I ask CEOs who we do business with how much time they themselves spend on selecting "the best and the brightest", the vast majority will answer that selection takes up no more than 5 to 10 percent of their time. Generally, they delegate this job to their HR director or possibly even to a corporate recruiter. Of course, there is nothing wrong with those employees. My point is that CEOs, leaders and managers need to realise that the recruitment of talent is absolutely crucial.

This insistence on the importance of recruitment from someone who has spent the better part of his career in **executive search** may not surprise you. But to repeat the aim of this book: it is a step-by-step plan, backed by theoretical data, geared at helping *you* do this job yourself in the future. Top talent recruitment requires the whole company to immerse itself in this quest. Managers can no longer delegate the selection of their team members; for companies to survive in today's turbulent environment, they must participate in the process as well.

Recruitment should not be limited to recruiters. It should be one of the key responsibilities of managers throughout the company. Decades ago, Jim Collins said he would always opt for recruiting the best possible staff if he had to choose between having a good strategy or recruiting the best staff. After all, having a good strategy without the proper people to implement it will surely negatively impact results. On the other hand, a team of excellent staffers is usually able to come up with and implement at least a half-decent strategy.

TRADITIONAL CRITERIA

I have noticed that most organisations opt to select their candidates based on their knowledge and abilities. The usual procedure is to skim through a candidate's experience, do an IQ test and assess skills. Next, they check a handful of references and may even verify that the person's degrees are real. These are all sensible steps – I would be the last to suggest that a good brain and a degree from a renowned university or business school are without merit. But they do not reveal the whole picture. If you want to home in on agile talent, you must do more. The insights provided by this book and its selection tools will help you in your selection of agile talent.

The Value of IQ

IQ is a rather important factor. In fact, it is one of the first markers of a candidate's ability to cope with change. Still, you should be wary of jumping to rash conclusions based on IQ. Almost without exception, all of the candidates we meet in our interviews are highly intelligent. Intelligence, then, is important, but it is by no means a distinguishing characteristic. Far more important is whether IQ is matched by other vital characteristics. These include having the right drive or motivational need as well as other personality traits. If these personality traits are absent, the predictive validity of IQ will not matter. It is a good jumping-off point, a valid first indication of merit, but it does not tell you everything you need to know. Besides, different types of intelligence are gaining traction and interest – more about this later.

"Without motivating energy, top talent will never achieve top results. Nor can a superb level of motivational drive make up for a lack of potential for top talent."

ROB VINKE, PROFESSOR OF HUMAN RESOURCE STUDIES, NYENRODE BUSINESS UNIVERSITY

47

CLEVER AND STILL UNSUITABLE

When people discuss intelligence, they often ask me if a talented person can be *too* clever. I don't think so, in principle. In virtually every field, a good intellect will come in handy. Still, the question is a valid one. People who are brilliant need to ensure that the rest of the world understands their insights or perspectives. This is particularly true of managers.

At the very core of modern management is a manager's ability to create the right circumstances for other people to succeed. A second prerequisite is a capacity to mobilise employees. It never ceases to amaze me how some managers can get others to jump through burning hoops, while others need to drag their staff by their hair. Being an effective manager has many facets, but the ability to get one's message across in a clear and simple way is certainly an essential one.

After all, it is one thing to be brilliant, but if that leaves staffers and managers who report to an executive completely baffled by his oracular pronouncements, that brilliance will only complicate matters. If people have no idea what an executive wants to achieve with his proposed solution or change of direction, they will refuse to follow his lead. In my book on top talent I discuss this topic at length in the chapter on reducing complexity. It all comes down to an ability to simplify things: it is the average and mediocre talents and managers who are inclined to over-complicate matters. The reverse happens less frequently. Having a person with an exceptionally high IQ as a manager will only work if that person brings along refined communication skills and a great deal of empathy.

Experience Often Overrated

It is not just IQ that is frequently overrated. Experience and knowledge are treated with the same undue deference. Yes, it is helpful if someone knows the tricks of the trade in their field, or has exceptional management acumen. In fact, when selecting candidates most businesses put experience at the very top of their wish list. They also demand a certain level of education. A wealth of experience, however, may prove to be counterproductive if it has made the potential hire resistant to change and reinvention. This is a recipe for disaster in today's world. No longer is experience the be-all and end-all; other facets have become more important. We will return to this topic later on.

We all know people who graduated with honours, yet who stumbled into mediocrity in their careers. The reverse is also true: there are scores of successful entrepreneurs who have reached the highest ranks yet do not boast a degree.

When I think of university degrees, my mind always goes to Steve Jobs, the late chief of Apple. In his spectacular 2005 commencement speech at Stanford University,* Jobs was perfectly open about not having a college degree himself. In fact, he was a college drop-out. In his speech, the Apple executive insists the next generation should not make the same mistake. He tells them that the road to the top will be that much easier to navigate when you have gone through the proper education. Still, Jobs does acknowledge that his blend of other characteristics helped him achieve all that he did.

"As you move up through a company, you will notice executives increasingly distancing themselves from recruitment. In fact, this ought to be the reverse."

ERIC SCHMIDT & JONATHAN ROSENBERG, GOOGLE

---

* You can watch the video *Steve Jobs Stanford Commencement Speech 2005* on YouTube.

THE MYTH OF THE DROP-OUT ENTREPRENEUR

The Kaufmann Foundation recently presented research backing up the advice of Steve Jobs when he told students to finish their college degrees. The foundation focuses on research regarding entrepreneurial spirit and the improvement of education for young people. It discovered a significant correlation between the kind of education an entrepreneur obtains and the success of their startup businesses. The research looked at over 500 high-tech companies founded between 1995 and 2006 in the United States. The vast majority of founders of these businesses had advanced degrees. Startups founded by entrepreneurs with lower levels of education turned out to be significantly less successful. Yes, Steve Jobs, Mark Zuckerberg and Bill Gates reached great heights without any diplomas or degrees, but they are absolute exceptions to the rule.

To sum up: a college degree and a person's IQ do indeed have some predictive validity, and should be taken into consideration by prospective employers. But a better prediction of success is achieved by adding other elements to your screening of candidates.

For the very reason that having an advanced degree only provides so much information, Google pays scant attention to degrees when they select talent. The company does value the skills and experiences acquired by college students, but the actual degree tells the company little about how talented a person is, or the level of their grit and determination. After all, it cannot tell you if someone achieved it through an immense amount of hard work, or by winging it and participating in a wide range of extra-curricular activities. Nor does it let you discover what other relevant characteristics a person has. Is he any good at speaking in front of a large group of people? Can he motivate others? Is he capable of conceptual out-of-the-box thinking, or did he just pass all his exams and write all his papers by rote? It makes sense to take all of these considerations into account in drawing up your selection criteria.

Perfectly Competent But Not So Perfect After All

I believe that the limitations of selection based on skills and competence are made clear when we consider the business disasters of recent years, in both the public and the private sector. Enron is one such dramatic example, as are various well-known startling events at Dutch retail and housing businesses, not to mention a college for advanced education in the Netherlands. The dramatic failures emanating from the top of an organisation were rarely caused by incompetence or a lack of skills on the part of the top executive. Generally, the top managers of these failed companies were very intelligent, highly experienced and competent people. However, some of them had a personality type which could be described as narcissistic or megalomaniac. Personality disorders such as these can lead a CEO or chairman to endanger a company in a specific set of circumstances.

These examples make one thing obvious: it is essential to screen top executives for their personality and motivational needs. In the chapter dealing with Step 2 or people's motivational needs, we will examine this need at length.

AMBIGUOUS CONTEXT

Apart from limiting selection to IQ, skills and experience, another reason why a company's selection procedure falls short is when they fail to specify the situation the organisation operates in and consequently to articulate what it requires of the candidate. One side of this story is that selection is not being tailored to the particular wishes and needs of the organisation and the team in which the new hire will be working. The other side is that when someone has shown exceptional performance at one organisation, everyone assumes they are automatically qualified to be equally successful in a range of other organisations. In reality, it does not follow that success in one domain automatically translates into success in another. Step 1 is a discussion of how to change this and how to canvass the context of an organisation.

UNSTRUCTURED INTERVIEW

The third way to mess up the selection process is to conduct unstructured interviews with candidates. What this means is that the interviewer asks all manner of serious questions on a range of topics, but without prior preparation for the interview. Preparing for an effective interview involves a distinct and detailed outline of which skills, personality traits and motivational needs the candidate must have, to be considered for the position. If an interview is unstructured, there is a very real danger of trying through the questions to confirm a positive first impression. Psychologists refer to this process as confirmation bias. Steps 3 and 4 will explain how to avoid these pitfalls, no matter how understandable they might be.

ALARM BELLS OUT OF ORDER

Some situations occurring during the selection process should trigger the proverbial alarm. Here are several difficulties I have come across frequently over the years.

I have just referred to the important ability to make complicated things sound simple. But what should you do with someone who does the exact opposite? If you come across someone in a selection interview who seems to make things complicated for no reason, I suggest you take time to find out why. The candidate might be trying to hide something, or wish to paint a more positive personal picture than is justified. Or maybe the person is bluffing to cover a lack of the required experience with the topic you are discussing.

The opposite sometimes occurs too: a person provides an excellent, relevant analysis but cannot articulate it in straightforward, understandable language. There are many guises that this behaviour comes in: overusing jargon, regurgitating "soundbites" from popular management books, or answering in general terms when the question was highly specific. Should you run into candidates exhibiting this fault, be sure to ask them to clarify their answers, or confront them with their odd behaviour. Their perhaps overly-defensive response will tell you what you need to know about their tendency to overcomplicate things.

I notice that the most talented people rarely have this overcomplicating tendency. Instead, their ability to present things in a clear and concise manner sets them apart.

Another instance that should set off the recruiter's alarm bells is when candidates exhibit widely differing behaviour depending on whom they are speaking to. I have often come across candidates who were perfectly polite and pleasant to the interviewer, yet displayed a stiff, grumpy or rude manner when they spoke to the receptionist. If you notice behaviour of this type, make sure to find out more: someone who is patronising or worse to his perceived underlings because he believes they do not deserve to be treated kindly, is not going to be the right person for the job. As a rule, you should be looking for emotionally stable people whose integrity manifests itself in large and small matters.

Professor Erik van de Loo, who teaches Leadership & Behaviour at TIAS Business School and Organisational Behaviour at INSEAD, believes this type of behaviour is a warning sign regarding people who behave differently among their peers and superiors, as against how they behave with others they deem inferior. I now check how each candidate behaves towards my personal assistant. Anyone who is snappish and uncivil for no apparent reason can hardly be considered suitable for a position of leadership.

USING A VARIETY OF SELECTION TECHNIQUES
Research has taught us that using a variety of selection techniques will in fact produce a better prediction of future suitability. Based on this, we should make use of several different tools and tests in our selection of talent.

In 1998, the American researchers Frank L. Schmidt and John E. Hunter conducted research into selection techniques and their predictive validity. Their meta-analysis held particular merit on account of its summation of the wealth of global research conducted over the previous 85 years.

These scientists were especially interested in mapping out the predictive validity of various selection techniques. In other words: how reliable and valid are the selection methods that were applied, and to what degree – on average – do they manage to predict a candidate's future behaviour in any given position? Schmidt and Hunter examined the prevalent selection techniques and were able to conclude that some tools have a rather significant degree of predictive validity. One example of such a tool is the focused or "criterion-based" interview which produces far better results than an unstructured open interview, which lacks focus on the essential criteria for the position under consideration. Other aspects, including the number of years of advanced education and experience, have proved to be far less accurate predictors. Significantly, the research makes clear that the more structured and systematic the use of a selection tool/technique is, the greater its predictive validity. Furthermore, Schmidt and Hunter concluded that the average validity of a selection tool's prediction is strongly influenced by the level of expertise of the recruiter. The research is not merely limited to tools measuring IQ, skills and knowledge. It also concerns itself with the predictive validity of personality traits. Echoing Schmidt and Hunter's vision of a properly rationalised combination of selection tools, I would personally stress the importance of using selection tools which offer a reliable evaluation of a candidate's motivational needs. In doing so, you will produce a more panoramic picture of the candidate and his possible future behaviour. In Appendix 1, you will find an overview of their research findings.

CONCLUSION

Evidently, businesses and their employees will have to become more agile as time passes. How we currently select talent comes up short, as we have discussed in some depth. And this failure to select appropriate talent can have serious repercussions in the business world, as we have seen. Even though the old familiar criteria will never be completely reduced to rubble, the impact of technological innovation and the speed of change will have a profound and lasting effect on the field of selection. Everything you know, everything you can do, everything you have achieved in the past, all of that will not be decisive in the future. What really matters is the ability to adapt to completely new situations. Eagerness to learn new things, to show resilience and determination during unexpected challenges are good indicators of that adaptability.

A blend of personality traits and motivational needs will then become the most important measures used in selecting talent. In particular, being able to discern the right need (for achievement), curiosity, resilience, creativity, determination, inspiration, understanding and learning ability will decide the selection of agile talent. The focus when selecting agile talent will not be on the skills someone already has, but rather on their ability to understand, cope with and solve the questions and dilemmas of tomorrow, the day after and the days to come.

In the next section of the book, I will describe three separate stages consisting of nine steps in total, which will provide you with a winning combination for selecting agile talent.

FURTHER READING

BOOKS

- Lance Berger & Dorothy Berger (2010). *The Talent Management Handbook. Creating a Sustainable Competitive Advantage by Selecting, Developing, and Promoting the Best People.* McGraw-Hill Education.
- Angela Duckworth (2016). *Grit. The Power of Passion and Perseverance.* Scribner.
- Sydney Finkelstein (2016). *Superbosses. How Exceptional Leaders Master the Flow of Talent.* Portfolio.
- Kimberly Janson (2015). *Demystifying Talent Management. Unleash People's Potential to Deliver Superior Results.* Maven House.
- Lidewey van der Sluis, Sylvia van de Bunt-Kokhuis, and others (2009). *Competing for Talent.* Koninklijke Van Gorcum.

ARTICLES

- Talya N. Bauer (2010). *Onboarding New Employees: Maximizing Success.* SHRM Foundation.
- eFinancialCareers (February 2012). *How to Avoid Hiring Disasters.* Whitepaper.
- R.J. Sternberg (1997). "The Concept of Intelligence and Its Role in Lifelong Learning and Success." *American Psychologist*, 52 (10), pp. 1030-1037.
- Vivek Wadhwa, Richard Freeman & Ben Rissing (May 2008). *Education and Tech Entrepreneurship.* Ewing Marion Kauffman Foundation.

PART 2. SELECTING TOMORROW'S TOP TALENT

"Talent is the currency of the new economy."

LIZ WISEMAN

By default, selection is determined by several elements. This is why no single person will ever be a 100 percent match. Subjecting everyday selection practices to a thorough check is a smart move, leading to improvements and adjustments. We should further bear in mind that what was once required of talent, and what we ask of agile talent today, are two very different things.

In this section of the book, I will tap into my practical experience in this field, giving ideas for selecting future-proof talent. I will not waste any time discussing worn-out familiar topics. Instead I will focus on those issues that frequently lead to problems or are often overlooked. I am guided by two questions: what can we change and how can we do a better job?

I have teased and tinkered with my methods of selection over the years, adding elements, discarding others, constantly making improvements. But I don't consider this method of mine to be etched in stone. Why don't you try out my method? You will find out what works for you and how blending and seasoning the ingredients will enable you to achieve your very own recipe for selecting talent.

THREE CONSECUTIVE STAGES, WITH NINE STEPS IN ALL

My method for selecting agile talent consists of nine steps carried out over three consecutive stages: the preparation, the actual selection and the verifying of conclusions. Some of the steps are consecutive, but within a stage they do not necessarily need to be completed in the suggested order. The steps are not all equally agile, but they are all essential. It is the combination of all the steps that produces a better selection of future-proof talent.

STAGE 1: **PREPARATION**

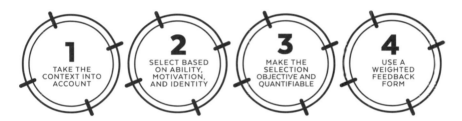

STAGE 2: **SELECTION**

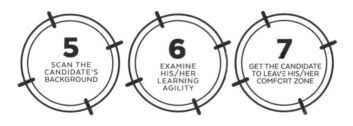

STAGE 3: **VERIFICATION**

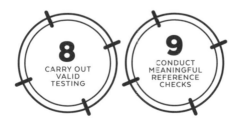

If you are serious about improving your selection process, I strongly urge you to follow all the nine steps. You will no longer base your judgment on one or two of the steps, or inadvertently place a higher value on any one of them. Besides, it does not make sense to carefully examine some aspects of a candidate, but disregard others.

Instead, it is more sensible to take a serious and thorough approach to each step of the selection process and to assess them together as a whole, instead. This is the way to significantly increase the odds of a successful match. My own practical experience is not the only reason I can vouch for this; there is a wealth of research, including the findings of the aforementioned Schmidt and Hunter, which says the exact same thing.

Selecting people will never be an easy job, but the nine simple steps are bound to improve the odds of a successful match and to minimise your need for outside advice.

STAGE 1. PREPARATION

The idea of preparation being key may seem self-evident. Sound preparation involves a consensus among the people involved in the selection process. What are they looking for? Deciding on clear and unambiguous criteria is next, to ensure that all the relevant people are on the same page. This will help boost the objectivity of the selection process and make it more measurable.

This stage consists of four crucial steps:
- Take the context into account.
- Select based on ability, motivation, and identity.
- Make it objective and quantifiable.
- Use a weighted **feedback form**.

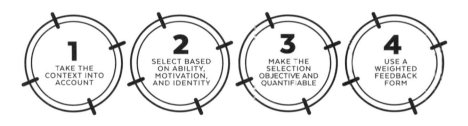

STEP 1. TAKE THE CONTEXT INTO ACCOUNT

"Sometimes your greatest strength can emerge as a weakness, if the context changes."

HARSHA BHOGLE, INDIAN CRICKET COMMENTATOR AND JOURNALIST

One of the very first steps you need to take when you start selecting talent is to outline the prospective employee's new work environment. Another word for this is context. This is an essential step, because there is no such thing as universal skills and traits that will fit every single organisation or match each conceivable scenario. Unfortunately, too many organisations still regard top talent as a universally effective magic potion.

THE UNIVERSAL TALENT MYTH

The assumption that a highly talented person will succeed in any situation and every possible leadership role is inherently flawed. Often, be it in sports, business or politics, outliers succeed in the context of specific challenges paired with a particular set of conditions. In other words: they excel under certain circumstances and with a distinct group of people with complementary skills. A player who does well at Manchester United, may be less successful at Ajax, Chelsea or Barcelona. Similarly, a brilliant merchant banker at ING may not be nearly as successful at Goldman Sachs. A lot hinges on the person's talent in conjunction with the specific situation. Is the potential hire able to use his/her talent in this place and context? Will he or she be compatible with the strategy of the organisation, its purpose and culture, as well as with the blend of skills, personality traits and motivational needs of the other team members? All these factors make very specific demands on the potential hire. Besides, you should always ascertain whether or not the talent is up to the specific challenges your organisation is facing.

CONTEXT OUTLINED IN CHARCOAL

How do you map out if a candidate matches the particular challenges and prerequisites of the position? First off, you need to outline the circumstances of the organisation which is on the lookout for talent. What is its strategy? What is the company culture, what is the structure of management and governance? What kind of challenges and dilemmas is the organisation up against? Who are the key decision makers – influential employees apart from senior management and directors? What degree of independence are managers given? Are they basically highly trained implementers or are they expected to contribute to the company's strategic direction? Is it a mid-sized company with no real advisory staff to speak of, where employees are expected to have a practical hands-on mindset, along with their strategic conceptual vision?

Once you have finished this company chart, examine the combination of people already working there. What kind of skills do they bring to the table, what are their personality traits, what are the needs that motivate them? Who would best complement them?

In addition to all this, the needs and purpose of the candidate must be compared and matched to those of the organisation's purpose. If these are more or less in sync, you can be fairly sure of a good match between the two.

Next a clear picture, an "outside-in" view of the candidate and the organisation must be created. How to accomplish this? By making a scan which you either conduct yourself or delegate to a line executive or HR professional. The scan should cover these three topics:

1. The strategy and other contexts of the company
2. The company culture
3. The other employees within the organisation: the match within the team

STRATEGY AND OTHER CONTEXTS

In order to summon a better picture of the strategy and other company context, you would do well to dig deeper and sift through the business context (macro-level), operating context (meso-level) and, finally, the department or unit context (micro-level).

Macro-Level

An assessment of the macro-level or the business context must focus mainly on what the aim of the business is: in what field or business sector does the organisation operate, i.e. what business are we in? It is essential that you form a mental image of the markets, proposals, customers and sales channels which all play a crucial part in operating the business.

Meso-Level

An assessment of the operating context needs to examine how the business manages to succeed. I encourage you to look at these elements:

- The company purpose. What is the higher purpose of the organisation, or why are we here?
- The company values. What does the organisation believe in, what is its value set? For example: "We do our work with integrity, we focus on cooperation, we inspire others through leading by example, and we communicate both internally and externally in an open and honest manner."
- The company vision. What does the company aspire to be?
- The company strategy. What methods is the company employing to achieve its goals?
- The company promise. How do we want the world to see us?

Micro-Level

An assessment of the department/unit context will consider how much impact the desired agile talent is likely to have, and whether or not the person will fit in. Here, you should check out aspects such as:

- Who will the person be working with? What do these people bring to the table in terms of ability and identity? What drives them?
- Who are the managers? What do they contribute with respect to skills and identity? What drives them?
- Who are the key customers, both within and outside the company?
- What are the financial ambitions and other goals for the unit/department?
- What are the key innovations?
- What important change paths are scheduled?

"It ultimately boils down to this: that you will be able to match the knowledge, personality and motivational needs of the talent to the culture, strategy and purpose of the organisation!"

The answers to these questions provide va uable information as to what others bring to the table. Now, you can assess whether the talent you have selected will complement current staffers regarding knowledge, experience, drive and personality. In fact, without this information you are clueless as to what kind of person is a good match, and you cannot effectively embark on the selection process! It is only after you have determined what the company is and where it is headed, and you have assessed who the candidate is and what drives him/her, that you can make a proper match.

If the position you are hoping to fill already exists (i.e. someone is leaving), then you need to do a micro-level context assessment to ascertain if the previous person was or was not successful in that position. This assessment can supply valuable information for the future candidate's performance in that role.

CULTURE

After answering the questions on operating context and unit context, your picture of company culture will start to come into focus. To help you fine-tune your information, I have provided several ideas under "Further Reading" at the end of the chapter.

One of the most prominent authors on management, specialising in cultural differences, is Fons Trompenaars, a Dutch-French organisational theorist, management consultant, and author in the field of cross-cultural communication. His authoritative work *Riding the Waves of Culture* is built on the premise that "if something works in one culture, there is little chance that it works in another." Trompenaars stresses that it is important to accurately chart the company culture before assuming that the talent in question is going to fit in perfectly. Delving further into the subject, Trompenaars joined forces with Charles

Hampden-Turner to draw up a cultural model which distinguishes between seven different dimensions of culture. In addition, he developed the "Culture for Business" app which lets you use that model to paint a fairly accurate picture of a company's culture. A new app is currently in development, called "Career for Business". This app promises to help you chart the match between a candidate and the organisation.

Not every place you fit in is where you belong

© Liesbeth Houtman

THE MATCH WITHIN THE TEAM

A frequent selection pitfall is the tendency to make a match based on a candidate's personal profile instead of one matching a successful member of the team. Often someone who leaves an organsation (aside from retiring or being lured by a major promotion elsewhere) does so based on a bad fit with the other team members. A poor fit is based on a fundamental error of matching the candidate with the position, not the team. Clearly, a match with the position is relevant, but it is equally important to determine whether someone fits in with the other key players within the organisation. Key players include the management and also others who exert a significant influence on company affairs. Are these people even mildly in sync with one another or might conflicts be simmering below the surface? Do their personalities complement each other, or do they share many overlapping personality traits and abilities?

"People have widely varied profiles, which may or may not produce the best results under any given circumstances, or in any situation or context."

HENK BREUKINK, SUPERVISORY BOARD MEMBER
AND EXECUTIVE COACH

I strongly urge you to spend serious time figuring out who are the most important people within the organisation. This sleuthing should give you a good idea about their abilities and personalities as well. You need to be wary of simply hiring clones of the current management and employees. Instead, you should craft a team of mutually complementary individuals. While many businesses claim to do so, in practice they have great difficulty following through with this ideal.

Actually, people are naturally inclined to do exactly the opposite of this. Virtually everyone who has not been trained to watch out for homogeneity is inclined to take themselves as a benchmark and end up hiring people who are extremely alike. This psychological phenomenon is called similarity attraction.

A variation on this theme is when someone hires a candidate who may look completely different, though in fact the new hire closely resembles the current management team. One instance of this "different-but-the-same" phenomenon would be a manager with an immigrant background, who has assimilated to the new culture to the point of abandoning his original heritage. You might be able to forestall this problem by making clear what your selection criteria will be (steps 2 and 3) and by objectifying and measuring those criteria, through the use of a weighted feedback form.

Over a decade ago, Boris Groysberg and several others at Harvard University did extensive research into top talent moving between positions in the world of finance. A key discovery was that candidates often experienced a slump in their performance after moving to a different company. The academics were certain that this was caused by their achievements being highly dependent on their interaction with others, which the move perhaps temporarily disrupted, as well as the company culture and their personal network of contacts. In fact, when it was not one highly talented individual but a whole team that switched to another organisation (this is fairly common in finance, accountancy and law), the negative effect was far less profound, sometimes to the point of being negligible.

CONCLUSION

After scoping out the context from company level to culture and team, you are ready to get started on the criteria which a candidate needs to meet. We have already seen that it is essential to look beyond IQ and experience, and to include those criteria befitting agile talent. Next, you can move onto composing a job description which takes the situation into account and – ideally – will generate a match compatible with the team. While writing up job descriptions is important, this activity does not fall within the scope of this book.

FURTHER READING

BOOKS

- R. Meredith Belbin (2010). *Team Roles at Work*. Elsevier Science Ltd.
- R. Hogan & J. Hogan (2009). *Hogan Development Survey Manual* (2nd Edition). Hogan Assessment Systems.
- Fons Trompenaars & Charles Hampden-Turner (2012). *Riding the Waves of Culture. Understanding Cultural Diversity in Business*. McGraw-Hill Education.
- Fons Trompenaars & Piet Hein Coebergh (2015). *100+ Management Models. How to Understand and Apply the World's Most Powerful Business Tools*. McGraw-Hill Education.

ARTICLES

- Jean Martin & Conrad Schmidt (May 2010). "How to Keep Your Top Talent." *Harvard Business Review*.

STEP 2. SELECTION BASED ON ABILITY – MOTIVATION – IDENTITY

"You are hired for your abilities and fired for who you are."

HENK BREUKINK, SUPERVISORY BOARD MEMBER AND EXECUTIVE COACH

Part 1 dealt with the need to screen candidates for more than "just" their abilities and knowledge. After all, in addition to someone's experience, skills and IQ ("ability"), their motivational needs ("motivation") and personality traits ("identity") are becoming increasingly important to their future success. As we move away from traditional kinds of intelligence, we are starting to make additional demands apart from IQ and to take into account EQ, for emotional intelligence and AQ, which highlights adaptability, are gaining ground. Step 6 then will be a separate section on learning agility.

IQ ⟶ EQ ⟶ AQ

TRADITIONAL INTELLIGENCE   SOCIAL INTELLIGENCE   ADAPTIVE INTELLIGENCE OR ADAPTABILITY

SHIFTS IN INTELLIGENCE TYPES

A report by the Davos 2016 World Economic Forum estimates that within the next five years, 35 percent of the skills which are crucial today will change profoundly. I actually believe this may be a conservative estimate and the true number will prove to be higher.

The research I reviewed and my own practical experience prompt me to suggest you add two extra dimensions to the traditional qualities of "can" and "know" when you select agile talent. You should also take into account what motivates and drives people, and review who they are – their personality.

THREE KEY FACTORS

When you select agile talent, remember to bear in mind what I have condensed into three factors: ability, motivation and identity. Each forms an axis and they are the basis for your selection. When I mention "ability" I am referring to experience, skills and IQ – the traditional characteristics of knowledge and capacity. I will discuss these three factors according to their increasing degree of complexity.

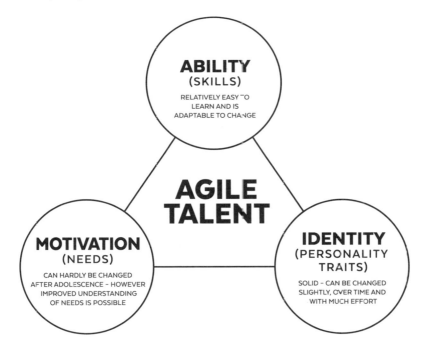

ABILITY
(SKILLS)
RELATIVELY EASY TO
LEARN AND IS
ADAPTABLE TO CHANGE

AGILE TALENT

MOTIVATION
(NEEDS)
CAN HARDLY BE CHANGED
AFTER ADOLESCENCE – HOWEVER
IMPROVED UNDERSTANDING
OF NEEDS IS POSSIBLE

IDENTITY
(PERSONALITY TRAITS)
SOLID – CAN BE CHANGED
SLIGHTLY, OVER TIME AND
WITH MUCH EFFORT

THE THREE KEY FACTORS IN SELECTING AGILE TALENT

> ## "Within five years, a staggering 35 percent of today's crucial skills will change profoundly."
>
> *THE FUTURE OF JOBS* REPORT, WORLD ECONOMIC FORUM, 2016

Ability (and Knowledge)

Each of us has our own idea of what we mean by the term *ability*, but the variations boil down to what people know and what they are capable of. For example, we refer to the *ability* to properly conduct an interview with a candidate. Similarly, we all know what we mean by knowledge as a subset of ability. We immediately come up with examples such as fluency in a foreign language, playing a piece by Mozart or reciting long passages from Shakespeare.

Identity

A discussion of personality traits is where things start to get complicated. Broadly speaking, these traits denote who you are, the virtues and habits that distinguish you as a person. A kaleidoscope of characteristics comes to mind, rarely bundled in any individual: perseverance, determination, meticulousness, emotional stability, extroversion, resilience, creativity, kindness. The list could be extended.

I believe that in a world in flux, the personality traits of adaptability and resilience, as well as the ability to learn and embrace change will become vastly more significant for the selection of the best talent than they are today. After all, these are unique characteristics which tend be fairly stable over time. They are robust and cannot be learnt or altered as easily as skills.

It is widely accepted in science that personality, like intelligence, is largely determined by genetics. From the time of puberty personality traits start to solidify and when a person hits thirty they are virtually set in stone. In other words, from then on it is extremely hard to change these traits, even when targeted directly by training or counselling. Smart candidates have probably been tweaking and sculpting these traits since the very beginning of their careers. Finding a suitable match between candidate and position based on the pertinent personality traits is one of the most important tasks in recruitment, since trying to change a trait is likely to prove a waste of time and energy. The motivational needs of a candidate present an even greater challenge. How to properly take motivational needs into account as you select the right candidate will be explored in step 8.

Personality traits can be analysed and even quantified and modified somewhat through extensive training. While there are many different ways to determine the nature of personalities, the so-called Big Five Test,* otherwise known as the Five Factor model, is widely accepted by psychologists and is generally regarded as one of the most accurate models for personality testing. This test scores a personality on five main dimensions: openness, conscientiousness, agreeableness, extraversion, and neuroticism.

Motivation

In addition to skills and personality traits, there is a third category to consider in selecting talent. This category is motivational needs or drives. I have been exploring the field of what motivates people for a while now, researching the topic at length for my book *How To Become CEO*. There are two distinct subcategories where motivation is concerned: motives (or rationales) and motivational needs.

Another way to describe motives is to refer to our value set, which is generally accepted and well-known. For this reason, I will limit the scope of this topic here to people's motivational needs. In part 3 we will revisit motives when we discuss the checklist provided by several CEOs and their subsequent evaluation of integrity as a selection criterion. I decided to delve deeper into the topic of needs, because it is less commonplace and calls for further clarification. Besides, it is a key factor when you are selecting agile talent.

Needs are notoriously hard to describe – rather the opposite of skills, in fact. There is no method that can perceive needs from the exterior. In adults, needs are essentially fixed and even more arduous to change than personality traits, which means you had better seriously keep them in mind during selection. Once you have selected someone, you have to make it work in harmony with their needs. You cannot make any significant alterations to a person after they have reached adolescence.

---

* P.T. Costa and R.R. McCrae designed the most frequently used questionnaire for this test, in 1992.

NEEDS CAN PREDICT BEHAVIOUR

Essentially, motivational needs are the innermost motives which drive someone to achieve a certain goal or situation. A metaphor may help explain how needs function in our lives: they tend to work like the battery charger in a car. In our everyday existence of interacting socially, we all need a source of energy to charge our inner battery. If you manage to satisfy one of your dominant needs, you will feel recharged and fulfilled. Our human battery can recharge itself. This works both ways: when you do things that are out of sync with your inner needs, you end up with an empty feeling of dissatisfaction. To stick with our metaphor, your energy supply can become drained to the point of depletion.

Needs tend to produce urges for action, with the strength of an urge varying with the dominance of the need. The blend of different interacting needs can affect the strength of an urge as well. A scholar who has conducted acclaimed research in this field is Harvard professor David McClelland. He has stated that needs or motivations are those things we spend the most time thinking about. His research shows that our way of thinking determines how we go about doing things, both at home and in our professional environment.

Boiling the research down, the reason is simple: if you rarely, or never, think about something, it is not likely that you will behave in a way that is in accordance with it. Vice versa, frequently thinking about something is often likely to produce behaviour that is in sync with your thoughts. McClelland and his peers assert that if you know what makes a person tick, you can broadly predict how this person is prone to behave.

Often, Though Not Always

Even though people largely behave according to their needs, there are reasons why these needs may not motivate action. A person's actions may be based on any number of things. For example, needing to display socially acceptable behaviour in a situation can be a constraint. In the long run though, needs absolutely and profoundly impact how people behave. Almost no one manages to stick to behaviour which is the polar opposite of their needs. This is why it makes sense to deepen your understanding of a candidate's motivational needs: your understanding can give you insights into how that particular person is likely to perform in the company, most of the time.

Under pressure, people are even more inclined to act according to their dominant needs. This is something we have learned from our life experiences

72

that is now supported by research. Of course, being able to predict how someone will behave under pressure is invaluable when evaluating a candidate's fitness for a job.

"Delving into the personality of the candidates is essential. An accurate personality profile will equip you with a deeper and richer understanding of the candidate's talent, and an improved grasp of his or her ability to excel at performing certain tasks. If you are eager to comprehend how a candidate might perform in particular position, you have no excuse to omit this aspect of talent from your selection."

The Impact of the Three Dominant Needs

In his research, David McClelland describes roughly 400 human motivational needs, lines of thought which influence your emotions and your deepest values. Three of these needs have such a profound effect on your social activities and your behaviour that the specialist literature terms them "primary social needs". McClelland has found they account for roughly 70 to 75 percent of all behaviour. They are the needs for achievement, affiliation, and power.

The Need for Achievement

The first of the primary social needs is the need for achievement. People with this particular need are extremely goal-oriented. They never stop thinking about how to improve their own performance and bolster their accomplishments. They feel energised and fulfilled by succeeding at difficult tasks and tough assignments. Frequently judging and evaluating themselves based on a standard of achievement they or an external entity (e.g. their company) set is second nature to them.

People with a strong need for achievement prefer working on assignments they are able to complete themselves, projects where they can exert the most influence on the outcome or result. Their satisfaction stems from creating results themselves, where their own performance defines the outcome. They never cease to look for ways to improve their own achievements and in the process, they frequently develop ideas for improving the speed or efficiency of work methods. Usually, people with a strong achievement orientation dislike routine jobs. They are creative and often feel drawn to innovation. Buzzwords that people motivated by the need for achievement employ are "invention" or "improvement". Their fierce love of accomplishing things themselves means they are – on average – slightly less inclined to keep in mind the perspectives or priorities of other people who might have other dominant needs. Generally, they are less adept at sensing and predicting the emotions of others. (Of course the degree of this perceived callousness depends on how much they are influenced by the other two primary social needs – we should be wary of blanket generalisations.)

On the whole, people with a strong need for achievement are eager to receive regular feedback. Regardless of whether this is positive or negative, feedback is a valuable tool for improving one's own performance.

Behaviour

People characterised by the need for achievement tend to have a strong competitive streak which imbues their every move and every thought. They love to do better than other people and they crave unique and eye-popping accomplishments such as being the first to finish, or setting a record for something. Impressing others is not a goal in itself; they are usually more interested in constantly raising their own bar. Achievement needs trigger people into a reflection on the long-term future of their career. Someone with a strong need for achievement might:

- keep on setting the bar higher, and higher yet
- want to achieve excellence and high quality in their performance
- want to win competitions
- seek accurate measurements of ongoing results, and ask for frequent feedback

Spotting Achievement-Dominant Candidates in an Interview

Motivational needs are best unearthed in a proper assessment, though there are little hints you may pick up during an interview. We have already determined that people with a need for achievement are eager to constantly improve. They will self-evaluate their behaviour during and after the interview, and love asking for feedback. Of course, people driven by the other needs may do so too, but the *achievers* will want to know all the ins and outs. They never let you get away with saying the interview was good or bad. They need specifics, detailed and well-reasoned feedback. They will ask questions in order to qualify, and are likely to ask for advice on how to improve those aspects that they need to work on. Even when their feedback is positive, they are eager to find out how to become better yet, or how to improve their efficiency. Nor will they avoid a heated debate during the interview, if they feel they might learn something. These are not people who take a wait-and-see attitude; instead they assess the interviewer to decide whether to take him seriously or not.

The Need for Affiliation

People with a need for affiliation are deeply committed to building and maintaining close friendships and strong relationships. For the most part, they are highly sensitive to other people. Virtually all those with this need have an acutely developed sense of empathy and finely-tuned feelers for the needs and emotions of others, especially of people close to them. They enjoy working with others and tend to dislike jobs which need to be done alone, or highly competitive tasks. Nor do they like their relationships to be tumultuous or disruptive. They will do anything to avoid conflict. Keeping relationships on an even keel is a top priority. Coping with criticism or negative feedback can be a challenge for them, whether in a personal or a working relationship. They can handle it, provided the group they are part of is given feedback but if they are singled out for individual feedback, they become uncomfortable. Often, they feel personally affected by feedback, interpreting it to mean "This person likes me," or "This person hates my guts."

The downside of this need is that when they sense no actual relationship with someone, they do not let them into their inner circle. As a result, people with a strong need for affiliation can be very dismissive of a person with whom they feel no relationship, to the point of completely ignoring this person. People characterised by the need for affiliation tend to despise large receptions and other events where only the most cursory and trivial social interactions take place. They would much rather spend time at intimate dinners or "private" parties with friends. Their family ties are often strong and they enjoy returning to their homes, where they can experience a deep sense of harmony and comfort.

Behaviour

People with a strong need for affiliation often reflect on how best to develop and maintain close relationships. They tend to prefer group activities to individual pursuits. Typical behaviour patterns for those with a need for affiliation are:

- helping other people with problems in their personal life
- putting themselves in someone else's shoes
- having an extremely friendly and trustworthy demeanour towards people at work

Spotting Affiliation-Dominant Candidates in an Interview

People with a dominant need for affiliation are genuinely interested in other people. They are truly keen to find out how someone else feels, and have acutely developed instincts to sense the preoccupations of others. This becomes obvious straight away in an interview – they are not asking questions for the sake of it, but aiming to build true connections. They prefer doing things as a group, rather than alone. If you ask about their personal achievements during an interview, you are likely to hear about the role of other group members played as well. They tend to avoid conflict and are eager to maintain a pleasant and constructive working atmosphere, even in an interview.

The Need for Power

People with a need for power are attracted to strength, influence and even authority over people and situations. They relish exerting influence over others and like to leave an impression of strength and toughness. "Power" can be a dirty word, when people award it negative connotations. That is why it is important to realise that power can simply mean "influence" and does not have to mean being a tyrant or an omnipotent ruler, terms which traditionally have been linked to power.

In general, people who are driven by the need for power tend to have exceptionally good social skills. They are always conscious of status symbols and all things prestigious. In the blink of an eye, they can sense the centre of power in an organisation. They reflect on their outward image and what impression they might be making on others. It depends on the version of their need whether these people prefer to wield actual influence over situations, or to do things which extend their influence. They might enjoy networking opportunities where they could meet important influencers, or become a mentor or coach to someone new to their field, or they might opt to take on voluntary board positions as a sideline. Later, I will discuss the separate versions of the need for power, as this need can be divided into a personal and a social version.

Behaviour

People with a strong need for power spend time reflecting on their position in relation to other people. Status and personal reputation are often very important to them. They enjoy being appreciated, valued and acknowledged. They are eager to have an impact on others. Broadly speaking, these people are capable of provoking strong emotions in others simply by how they conduct themselves. Someone with a strong need for power might:

- show plenty of initiative, take the lead;
- make decisions that not only affect themselves, but others too;
- tell others what they should be doing.

Spotting Power-Dominant Candidates in an Interview

People with a dominant need for power cut an impressive and strong figure during an interview. They are not the type for taking a wait-and-see approach – they will firmly show initiative. They show their decisive nature by candidly raising topics they wish to discuss, and they are not afraid of healthy debate, should it be necessary. The need-for-power orientation consists of four distinct stages. The main difference among the stages is between people with a personal need for power and those who are motivated by a social need for power. A person belonging to the former group is highly self-centred, often inclined to take full credit for a group achievement and knows when it is time to step into the spotlight. A person belonging to the latter group also takes to the limelight, but you can tell they have a sense of service to an organisation or a higher purpose. Their first objective is – genuinely – not power for its own sake.

The social versions of the need for power are individuals who are generally well-suited to leading agile talent. These are leaders who focus on others, are intent on motivating, inspiring and creating the perfect set of circumstances for other people to succeed in.

TWO SEPARATE VERSIONS: PERSONAL AND SOCIAL

The need for power is more complicated than the other two primary social needs. Research tells us that the need for power has many guises, depending on the person. There are four basic stages within this need. Stage one is generally viewed as the least developed, the least mature, whereas stage four is regarded as very rare and highly refined.

FOCUS OF POWER	ORIGIN OF POWER	
	OTHERS	SELF
SELF	STAGE 1 Dependent power	STAGE 2 Independent (autonomous) power
OTHERS	STAGE 4 Interdependent power	STAGE 3 Assertive power a. personal b. social

Source: Hay Group

THE FOUR STAGES OF THE NEED FOR POWER

The illustration of the four stages of the need for power is defined by the source and the focus of the power. In the first stage, the least developed one, the influence is drawn from others, and it is dependent power. That is the power from which a person draws inner strength: someone feels strong on account of their connection to a powerful person or organisation. You have undoubtedly encountered people who derive prestige or a positive sense of status from something outside themselves, for example a purser who works in business class for a distinguished airline, or a referee at an important football match.

The second stage of the need for power has people deriving power from within. This kind of power is not uncommon. This category could be defined as autonomous or independent power, where people use their own inner strength to inspire their actions, and their actions are basically self-oriented. While they dislike being told what to do, they are inclined to be authoritarian and controlling towards others. This is precisely why this category of people is not suitable for modern leadership. After all, agile talent does not perform too well under "control-freak" leaders and imposed guidelines. They prefer to be largely autonomous in the execution of their job. They will probably regard this kind of leader as uninspiring and authoritarian, who inhibits their own thinking and learning agility.

Although the third stage of the need for power also springs from within, this kind of power is harnessed to benefit others. The illustration shows us that this third stage has been subdivided into personal and social influence. Stage 3a refers to personal power: people who wish to feel better than others, or more influential. They are motivated by a need for personal power. At its most fierce, this type of behaviour could be described as "Sun King syndrome". They need the spotlight to be on them at all times, with their own achievements, results and goals eclipsing everyone else's. People with this particular orientation exude charm and charisma, which presents you with a challenge in weeding them out, unless you are familiar with this psychological category. On the other end of the spectrum, stage 3b or the stage of social power, these need for power people want to be devoted to a higher purpose. This may refer to an organisation focused on the common good, or to a mutually beneficial higher purpose between individuals. They are genuine in their pursuit of marshalling people to help them attain a specific goal or aid an organisation.

In the fourth stage of the need for power, the most mature and sophisticated of all, both the source and the target of power are external. These people are not self-centred where success is concerned. They often provide inspiration for others, making it possible for them to achieve their goals by being visibly motivated by a higher power instead of their own interests. For this very reason, all of us would ideally love to work for leaders of this calibre. They do not shy away from attention or leadership, but when they emerge as leaders it is never self-serving and always aimed at improving an organisation and its members or at re-alising a goal. You might think of Nelson Mandela or Mahatma Gandhi as examples of this stage.

Depending on how strong the presence of any one of the needs is in a person's psychological makeup, the individual will be more or less visibly influenced by it. It is important to realise that flesh-and-blood people are bound to be more complicated than the categorical types because the three dominant or primary motivational needs interact with each other and with the range of 397 other needs psychologist David McClelland identified (though some of these needs may be barely present in many people).

Two Examples

Here are two examples that will further clarify the three primary needs. Imagine going to play a round of golf with your three closest associates. You are all playing at the same skill range and a snapshot would show all of you looking like typical golfers. And yet it becomes evident that the behaviour of the players varies completely based on each of their dominant needs.

The first associate is guided by a need for achievement. As he plays golf, he is likely to focus on setting a new personal course record, or lowering his handicap. The second one has a strong need for affiliation. He enjoys playing with other people and feels that the atmosphere is far more important than the result of the game. Even having an off-day on the course, missing every single ball, he still says, "It was a great day today, we had so much fun together." The third associate has a need for power. His motivation during the game is beating everyone else and having them recognise him as the best player.

Another example: You and your team decide to go mountain climbing, up Mont Blanc or Mount Kilimanjaro, as an exercise in teambuilding. You have a clear objective, to reach the summit of the mountain together. On the way up the mountain the guide starts to realise that the group is made up of vastly different people. The first stage of the climb is uneventful – in fact, the man with the need for achievement is already thinking of his next summit, which has to be higher and more difficult to climb. After all, his orientation means he is always pushing himself to stretch his limits. Meanwhile, the teammate with a need for affiliation will be worrying about everyone managing to keep up during the whole climb, and is constantly checking to make sure no one gets left behind and – last but not least – everyone in the group is having a good time. The person with the need for power is fixated on how he will personally stick the flag in the ground at the summit, and then ask one of his mates to take a flattering picture of him. As they all climb back down the mountain, he starts to fantasise about giving an interview to *National Geographic* or a management magazine who would surely be interested in the climbing trip.

HOW TO BLEND CONTEXT WITH NEEDS AND PERSONALITY TRAITS

After completing step 1, a detailed map of what the context requires, you need to add to the mix the learning agility, self-confidence and areas of personal improvement required of the candidate. It also makes sense to consider risk factors or ingredients that threaten disaster: an excess of courage, a touch of paranoia or distrust, lack of emotion, refusal to take advice from someone, or being arrogant. They are all based in a blend of needs and personality traits.

People might fail as a result of their own personal risk factors, but being a bad match with the context or specific circumstances of an organisation is another road to failure. For that reason you should never stop at simply examining the talented individual, and instead always take the trouble of evaluating whether that person might fit in to the company context. That means that the start of every search for talent must be a detailed scan of the environment the candidate is going to be working in.

Peculiar Potential

It is equally important to match the current abilities and achievements of the candidate to the relevant criteria of the new position. This may sound obvious, but in reality a great many companies tend to assess how suitable someone is for a new job based upon their performance in their most recent position. It is a kind of laziness to assume that the excellent job someone did elsewhere makes them qualified for the demands of the job you are trying to fill. This very job could require an utterly different blend of skills and personality traits. It would be a mistake to consider current achievement with what one may achieve in the future.

A prime example is the successful salesman being promoted to Sales Director and subsequently failing. There are many more similar situations in which someone fails unexpectedly. Disaster often erupts when we fail to properly compare achievement and potential. Not taking the demands of the new environment into account is another toxic decision. Researchers Martin and Schmidt[*] believe these are issues which are often ignored in real life. Their research suggests that over 70 percent of today's high performers lack critical attributes essential to their success in future roles. One reason for this high percentage is that current developments are fast and fierce, both in speed and in impact on virtually all markets.

---

[*] Jean Martin & Conrad Schmidt (May 2010). "How to Keep Your Top Talent." *Harvard Business Review.*

"70% of today's high performers lack critical attributes essential to their success in future roles."

JEAN MARTIN AND CONRAD SCHMIDT, *HARVARD BUSINESS REVIEW*

This is made clear by the following case study, in which an excellent business unit manager at a large American company is moved to a new position. Based on his stellar record, the supervisory board asks him to step in as the CEO of a paint producing plant. However, his past achievements by no means guarantee a bright future.

EXPERIENCE VS. CONTEXT

This particular candidate had an outstanding track record in his field and had been highly successful at one of their key competitors for the past twenty years. The paint business was as familiar to him as the back of his hand, and he seemed to have the required experience in management. This man was known for his commitment to high quality and was universally appreciated by his staff. His sizeable business network was a further boost to his credentials.

Just as this new executive was starting out, the market entered a time of turmoil. The large multinational companies were suddenly joined by startups. Often mid-sized, these new entries on the market did more than simply focus on "making really good paint". They were very committed to sustainability and bursting with creative ideas. Besides, they had an out-of-the-box approach to prevailing business models. It turned out that they could not really be bothered with what the paint market had been up to in the past couple of decades. In fact, a lot of the top managers at these new businesses had no previous experience in this field. One of them had a background in education; another was an expert in medical biology. They set out to develop paint types which could be used in a variety of new situations, for example a paint-related product which could keep homes and schools cool in developing countries.

The new executive then learnt that many of his customers had signed up for a paint – developed by the competition – which could kill malaria mosquitoes and other insects. This product would be huge blow to his market share. In spite of his many good qualities, the new executive was not that brilliant at straying into unknown territory. He was inclined to stick to tried and true practices, the time-tested formula for eventual success. He saw no reason to adapt to change or new situations. At the company where he had been such a successful business unit manager, he had mostly been involved in the flawless execution of strategy devised by other people. Never before had he been expected to chart a new course for the business.

It was unfortunate that the HR manager had focused too strongly on listing the good qualities of this manager, instead of reviewing the key areas of improvement and personal development for the CEO in the course of the selection process. He also failed to examine what future demands the business might make on this executive.

For this very reason, you should always pay attention to what the specific potential for development is for any given candidate for a future position. As I mentioned before, what is required in terms of learning agility and development is by no means independent of the context. In reality, examining the potential for development is nothing more than making sure there is a match between what someone has already achieved, what you expect he or she will be able to achieve in the future along with the specific demands of the position for which he is being considered.

CONCLUSION

There are three completely different ways to play golf, or to climb a mountain, even though all the participants are simultaneously taking part in exactly the same activity. Being able to do a certain activity or job does, in actual fact, have no bearing on your motivational needs, nor on how these are likely to make you behave – this is particularly true under pressure.

Personality traits tell a similar tale. You might have two different CEOs lined up for an individual position, both of whom have a high IQ, an excellent track record and degrees from highly acclaimed universities. They are equally intelligent. Stressful situations then will determine which of these two will ultimately succeed.

It is wise to bear in mind that having succeeded in the past does not mean someone will succeed in the future. Taking the context into account is the smart thing to do; that is, asking where the candidate achieved his success and what is his potential for change.

FURTHER READING

BOOKS

- Ber Damen (2007). *Leiderschap en motivatie. Wat drijft en beweegt de topmanagers in Nederlandse organisaties?* Koninklijke Van Gorcum. Last chapter summary is in English.
- Daniel Goleman (1995). *Emotional Intelligence. Why It Can Matter More Than IQ.* Bantam Books.
- David C. McClelland (1978). *Human Motivation.* Cambridge University Press.
- David C. McClelland & David. G. Winter (1969). *Motivating Economic Achievement.* Free Press.

ARTICLES

- C.F. Aráoz (June 2014). "21st Century Talent Spotting." *Harvard Business Review.*
- A. Belasen & N. Frank (2008). "Competing Values Leadership: Quadrant Roles and Personality Traits." *Leadership & Organization Development Journal*, vol. 29, no. 2, pp. 127-143.
- Jean Martin & Conrad Schmidt (May 2010). "How to Keep Your Top Talent." *Harvard Business Review.*
- D.C. McClelland & D.H. Burnham (1976). "Power Is the Great Motivator." *Harvard Business Review*, 54(2), pp. 100-110.
- R.R. McCrae & O.P. John (1992). "An Introduction to the Five-Factor Model and Its Applications." *Journal of Personality*, 60, pp. 175-215.
- World Economic Forum (January 2016). *Global Challenge Insight Report. The Future of Jobs. Employment, Skills and Workforce Strategy for the Fourth Industrial Revolution.* World Economic Forum.
- S.J. Zaccaro (2007). "Trait Based Perspectives of Leadership." *American Psychologist*, vol. 62, nr. 1, pp. 6-16.

STEP 3. MAKE SELECTIONS OBJECTIVE AND QUANTIFIABLE

"We do not see things as they are. We see them as we are!"

HARRY FREEDMAN, AUTHOR AND ENTREPRENEUR

Any observation of people is bound to be complicated and somewhat biased. None of us has an objective, unbiased view of the world; our own frame of reference is a strong, though inadvertent influence. Positive and negative biases swirl around us, nudging our view this way and that. Decisions on the hiring or rejecting of talented individuals are governed by emotions, more often than not. Taking your intuition into account is fine, provided it is not the sole foundation for your decision. I would encourage you to never ignore your instinct. But remember: a gut feeling that for whatever reason gets skewed risks steering you towards a bad decision. If you have, say, an uneasy feeling about a candidate, you need to examine the facts more and find a rationale – solid data – to back up your uneasy feeling. So to underline an important point: it does not make sense to let gut instinct get the upper hand in the decision-making process. Decisions ought to be more rational, objective and quantifiable!

This chapter will cover two key methods for making objective and quantifiable selections:

1. Focused interviews
2. The principle of four eyes

FOCUSED INTERVIEWS

A focused interview is a structured interview. In it, you use a list of predetermined criteria to decide if a candidate is suitable for the position. You will have drawn up this list based on the job requirements, which become clear after outlining the company context. Time and again, research has proven that this kind of interview offers hugely improved predictive validity compared to unstructured interviews.

Highly experienced interviewers or recruiters will find this to be true, but those with little experience in selecting talent are likely to benefit even more. Inexperienced recruiters are far more inclined to be distracted by a candidate's exceptionally positive or negative qualities, even when these qualities are largely irrelevant to the future position and should not to be considered at all.

You might be tempted to think that there is little chance you would be distracted this way, but you would be seriously mistaken. In a matter of seconds, the first impression the candidate makes captures the interviewer's mind. The interviewer will then spend the rest of the session proving that impression, frequently using leading questions to do so. A negative first impression may stem from a limp handshake or from the candidate avoiding eye contact in the first few minutes of the interview. Positive first impressions might be equally shallow – having mutual friends or a shared interest in sports or other hobbies, for example. But what does a limp handshake have to do with an ability to think strategically and analytically? And how does having a mutual friend demonstrate the candidate's ability to execute a job?

While this kind of instant decision-making* has been proven to have almost no validity in predicting someone's future success, many interviewers are tempted to let their first impression be their guide. When the subsequent interview is unfocused, key criteria are likely to be completely overlooked.

The way to avoid this problem is to conduct a structured or focused interview. This type of interview helps you review the facts based on a set of criteria which you have decided upon in advance. Structured or focused interviews leave no room to evaluate the suitability of a candidate based on superficial and irrelevant criteria, be they positive or negative.

* The specialist term for this is "rapid cognition".

"It has been proven over and over that unfocused interviews offer poor predictions of how a candidate might perform in a future position, and yet they are still widely used."

Introspection and Adaptability as Indicators of Agile Talent

The STAR method is widely accepted as means to quiz a candidate on their approach to a *Situation*, asking them what their *Tasks* were, what *Action* they took and what *Result* it produced. Recently, the method has been amended to include *Reflection* or introspection: what did the candidate learn from the situation and do they have clear idea of their own strengths and of features that need improvement?

The traditional STAR method is a way to make a candidate use tangible achievements and successes to illustrate his role in what is often a team effort. The new version of the method does the same thing, with the addition of Reflection. Reflection is a relevant process to examine in more detail because of its positive effect on the ability to learn, so crucial to agile talent. Step 6 will provide an in-depth investigation of Reflection.

Moving beyond a simple examination of candidates' strengths and weaknesses is important and should include a review of their ability to learn from and reflect on experiences. Innovative talent and modern leaders never fail to pay close attention to reflection and introspection. Eager to analyse their own performance, experiences and mistakes, they consciously invite feedback. I therefore strongly suggest you include this key element in every interview. With agile talent in mind, I would furthermore encourage you to add the aspect of "adaptation" to the STARR method. How has someone demonstrably adapted to and implemented the lessons they learnt? On the one hand, adaptability is a key criterion in the selection of agile talent – this is a point this book drives home. On the other hand, you are keen to discover what someone has done to implement their reflection. After all, not adapting to what your introspection has taught you renders it useless. Therefore agile talent should demonstrate their capacity for introspection, and make clear how they put into practice the insights they uncover.

The following outline provides a brief overview of the steps in the updated STARRA-method.

Situation: what were the actual circumstances of this part of your working life? Who were your colleagues at the time and what was the context in which you worked together?

Task: exactly which tasks did you fulfil in this position? What were the key areas you were responsible for? What was expected of you? Which results did they assess your performance on?

Action: how did you choose your approach? What was your game plan? What actions did you take and which order did you follow?

Result: what was the result of you putting your plan into practice? How much of an impact did you personally have on the result? Which part of the result, good or bad, should be attributed to other team members or others within the company?

Reflection: what did this situation teach you? What would you do differently, based on what you know now? What did you learn about yourself? Based on that and with the future in mind, how will you need to adapt?

Adaptation: upon reflection, how did you adapt to and implement any changes? How have you moved beyond an analysis through reflection and introspection to implementing what you have learnt? Have you strengthened your approach through tangible and measurable behaviour changes or new ways of working?

STARRA-METHOD

How to Go About It

Traditionally, a focused interview will involve a discussion with others involved in the hiring decision – using a specific work situation as a talking point – of how suitable a candidate might be, how he fits the requirements and which skills and traits he possesses.

> The difference between an adequate match and an excellent one is defined, in 99 out of 100 cases, by the right soft skills: the unique blend of appropriate personality traits and needs. Aquent Staffing recently proved this once more in research across Europe.

When you have made up your mind to gather the input for the focused interview, your first move is a conversation with the manager or director who the future position will report to. Together you then discuss which traits are crucial for successfully executing the job. If you want to be thorough, you should speak with employees from the team which the position is part of and other relevant colleagues. Adding the input from the HR manager is another smart move. After all, the topic of motivational needs and personality traits is not generally the core business of line executives, so it makes sense to have an expert to help you dig up the essential criteria. Next, you discuss what the secrets for success are in this position. It boils down to these questions: what is the heart of this job and what does it take to do it well?

THE PRINCIPLE OF FOUR EYES

While structured interviews bring a degree of objectivity to the proceedings, multiple rounds of interviews involving several people in each round improve results even more. It makes sense to conduct interviews in pairs. Both interviewers can make up their own minds. It is useful to have a form to complete on which you score the candidate against criteria during the interview. Such a form also provides room for the selecting recruiter to write down observations. He should jot down his observations next to the relevant selection factor. This is the way to establish a focused observation method. It is important to have all the interviewers involved in the selection process fill out the feedback form as soon as possible after conducting an interview. Experience has taught us that after a couple of days most interviewers suffer serious memory lapses about the conversation. For this reason, we prefer to work with two interviewers for each conversation (the principle of four eyes) who take notes of what they observe as the interview takes place.

Filling out the form during the interview wards off the possibility of softening your judgment regarding a particular requirement or, conversely, making it more rigid because your judgment has been influenced by other factors. However, it is remarkably difficult to simultaneously observe, listen and write things down, and people tend to grossly overestimate their ability to multitask.

The Multitasking Myth
Initially, I found it extremely hard to observe and write at the same time. We tend to assume that we are perfectly capable of doing two things concurrently and remain focused on both, but the truth is less cut-and-dry. There is ample research to prove this.

Behavioural scientists at Warwick Business School have studied what goes on in our brain when we multitask. For instance, if we are conducting an interview and simultaneously writing down what we see, our brain activity simply switches back and forth rapidly between the two active areas. An article on the Dutch website of *National Geographic* (March 2013), states that multitasking does not exist as a phenomenon, "except for activities which we are highly proficient at, such as driving a car and listening to the radio, when the switch happens so rapidly that we do not notice it. An attempt to combine two less routine jobs changes this, however. The switch between areas of the brain slows down and hampers the execution of the activity." The result: a demonstrably higher occurrence of mistakes, even when people think this is not the case. Research into driving and talking on mobile phones has produced irrefutable proof of this.

Despite the wide acceptance among scientists that multitasking leads to more mistakes, many people are addicted to it. Our era of email, social media and smartphones is partly to blame, and some people even view their ability to multitask as a kind of status symbol.

At our office, we are convinced that even after intense training, you will be better at observing if you do one thing at a time. As a result, we always conduct interviews in pairs and alternate between asking questions and taking notes on our observations.

ASSEMBLING A SELECTION TEAM

During the final stages of preparation, you need to carefully consider how to assemble the selection team. A proper and thorough selection process should consist of three to four rounds of interviews, at the very least. If you take my advice to conduct the interviews in pairs, that adds up to a fair number of people. Apart from the appropriate manager, I always encourage my clients to include someone from HR on the selection team, together with several colleagues close to the position. This last step is referred to as peer selection. Immediate associates who will be working closely with the new hire are likely to be acutely aware of what it takes to do the job. It might also make sense to add a couple of staffers to the selection team for whom the future manager will be responsible. Despite the widely-held belief that you should not let people pick and choose their own manager, there are pertinent reasons to let them do just that. After all, these are the people who can determine if the candidate inspires. One of the key responsibilities for managers and leaders today is the ability to energise and be an inspiration to others. At Google, they have made the considered move to include a staffer from a completely different field in the selection team. This so-called cross-functional interviewer probably has little interest in filling that job, but does have a strong interest in keeping the quality of hiring high for the good of the company.

Finally, let me recommend that you always bring your best employees together in any selection team. In turn, they are sure to select the very best candidates. After all, the dictum that "A players select A players and B players select B or C players" may sound trite, but it is true.

SAVVY INTERVIEW QUESTIONS

Before conducting the actual interview, the interviewers should prepare thoroughly and decide what kind of questions they plan to ask. Even though a candidate's answer may do the job of eliciting follow-up questions, it helps to draft several basic questions in advance. This also precludes candidates being asked completely different questions, which could make for a more subjective comparison between them – exactly what you are hoping to avoid.

Which questions should you be asking and which ones should you leave out? Basically, there is no need to think up the most original questions. Instead, they should encourage candidates to reveal to you:

- who they are
- what they are motivated by
- how they work
- how they achieve things, and if they are willing to be candid about making mistakes
- if they take time to reflect, to plan, to adapt, before they jump into what they do next
- what their definition of success is and why

Here are some of my own tried-and-true interview questions, supplemented with several questions from Laszlo Bock, former senior vice-president of HR at Google, and Lou Adler, author of bestselling books *Hire with Your Head* and *The Essential Guide for Hiring & Getting Hired*. Both men have studied the field extensively.

Some possible interview questions:

- *Why do you want to leave your current employer?* I often pose this question, because it is enlightening to find out how people speak of their current position or manager. Someone who is excessively negative, who blames others for their own mistakes or who enjoys wallowing in self-pity is likely to repeat the pattern when you hire them at your company. At the very beginning of my career I made the mistake of taking someone like this on, and I have been wary ever since.
- *How do you set targets for yourself, and how do you go about reaching them? Using the STARRA-method, please show us how you work.* Superb candidates can give you a detailed and precise description of their ways of working. In fact, they instinctively share with you how much work they did and which part of the achievement was a team effort. They will spontaneously provide details about how they adjusted goals mid-project and what lessons they learnt along the way.
- *Could you share an incident where you clashed with someone, either an associate or a client? What caused the problem and what made working with them so hard? What did you do to resolve the situation? What effect did your actions*

have and what would you do differently, knowing what you know now? Again, it is not the conflict per se which is interesting, rather how it originated, whether or not there was a subsequent introspection process and how the problem was resolved.

- *When were you the most effective manager of your team, inspiring them to reach their goals? What was your plan and how did you ensure that individual and team targets were met?*
- *Which fact is missing from your resume, which you should have shared or want to share now? Why is that?*
- *Picture this: in an hour's time, you need to leave the office for an important client dinner, and you still have 250 unanswered emails clamouring for attention. How do you solve this dilemma?* The answer here can give you some idea of their problem-solving ingenuity and their ability to set priorities.
- *What is your greatest work achievement to date? Please share with us how you planned it, how you executed the job, what method you used to measure your success and what your worst mistakes were.* This question, devised by Lou Adler, gives candidates the opportunity to tell you about several aspects of themselves. You can find out how they work and plan things, how high they set the bar, and how they describe success. Also, you will learn of their willingness to acknowledge and take responsibility for their own failures.

On the other hand, there are questions which are better not asked at all, because they do not further your knowledge of the candidate or his/her introspective abilities. Other questions might be so obvious that every candidate will have prepped for them, leaving you with a stack of routine answers. Leading questions should also be avoided. Whenever you ask people if they have "a lot of empathy" or "good management skills", nearly everyone will say they do. The best way to refine your perception of someone is by asking open-ended questions pertaining to the core selection factors, letting the candidate give you examples and then comparing these to your own observations.

FURTHER READING

BOOKS

- Dave Crenshaw (2008). *The Myth of Multitasking. How "Doing It All" Gets Nothing Done.* Jossey-Bass.
- Edward M. Hallowell (2007). *CrazyBusy. Overstretched, Overbooked and About to Snap!* Random House Publishing Group.
- Ceri Roderick & Stephan Lucks (2010). *You're Hired! Interview Answers: Brilliant Answers to Tough Interview Questions.* Trotman.
- Shally Steckerl (2013). *The Talent Sourcing & Recruitment Handbook.* WEDDLE's.

ARTICLES

- Laszlo Bock (April 7, 2015). "Here's Google's Secret to Hiring the Best People." *Wired.* Extract from his book *Work Rules!* (2015).
- Ben Slater (April 28, 2016). "5 Interview Questions That Actually Help You Hire." Eremedia.com.

STEP 4. USE A WEIGHTED FEEDBACK FORM

"If you change the way you look at things, the things you look at change."

WAYNE DYER, AUTHOR AND PSYCHOTHERAPIST

After years in the recruitment field I have come to believe that the proper theoretical background and sufficient practice can help anyone improve their selection skills. All that is required is an interest in recruitment paired with a willingness to examine several crucial stages of the selection process. Most of these steps are hardly rocket science. Still, two elements do require slightly more attention than the others.

We have already covered one of these – motivational needs – in step 2. It is not difficult to acquire basic knowledge of what makes people tick. The hard part is strengthening your grasp of how the primary social needs work. Understanding the four stages of the power need does require serious and concentrated consideration. The second element which requires more attention is the weighting of the selection criteria. These are the five or six skills, personality traits and motivational needs we discussed in the previous chapter. These criteria were assembled as a joint effort of the selection team and lay the foundation for your focused interview.

CRITERIA ARE NOT EQUALLY SIGNIFICANT

Generally, criteria are not all equally significant or compelling when you are filling a position, which is why it makes sense to apply weighting. The best time to do this is at the session for deciding the actual criteria. That means your reasons and deliberations are still top of mind, and all the relevant people are assembled together. If you want to do this job well, be sure to include immediate associates and team members in the discussion in addition to the relevant manager. Ask the assembled group to list the key success factors on a scale of 1 to 5, in ascending order of importance: 1 is the least important requirement, whereas 5 is an essential prerequisite for the position.

As a rule, two or three of the (five or six) requirements will score a 5. Preferably, you should be compelled to strongly differentiate between the requirements, thus avoiding the temptation to award the bulk of them average significance. Ideally, a couple of them should only score 1 or 2. When people first start working with this method, they find it hard to vary the weighting of the requirements or criteria. Nor do they succeed in reaching a consensus straight away.

Search and recruitment is not possible though, if you do not reach some level of consensus. This often leads to people abandoning the entire idea of weighting, opting to stick to the criteria.

I think it is wiser to at least categorise the criteria and slightly discriminate between them. Organisations that take this approach usually limit the categories to must-haves and nice-to-haves. Over the years, I have come to understand that *two* categories are insufficient. I believe you should separate the must-haves into two additional subcategories, which I will discuss at length a little later. Another important step is to include a category for obstacles. I have encountered several candidates who fit the bill perfectly, yet I was adamant that I would on no account introduce them to our clients. This might have been because they lacked integrity or appeared untrustworthy, or because their personalities seemed likely to provoke trouble.

At work, I use three categories to discriminate among the pertinent criteria:
- foundation factors or non-negotiables
- obstacles or deselection factors
- core selection factors, the most critical for selection

Foundation Factors

Until a decade ago, I would just distinguish between the must-haves and the nice-to-haves when I considered requirements a candidate should meet. However, I came to realise that this distinction was not sufficiently sophisticated in most cases. I decided to make some improvements and went on to discuss the topic with many different experts in the field. One stood out for me: John Beeson, the American executive coach and management guru who has meticulously investigated this topic. When I met him in 2012 in New York, where I was interviewing him for the introduction to the Dutch version of his book, we had a rich and vivid discussion on how to categorise criteria. In his book *The Unwritten Rules: The Six Skills You Need to Get Promoted to the Executive Level*, Beeson divides the must-haves into two separate categories: the non-negotiable or foundation factors, and core selection factors. He believes every single attempt at categorising begins with the foundation selection factors. These are the essentials a candidate must have to be considered for the position. For instance, someone cannot be eligible for an executive position of leadership if their track record is anything short of stellar, or if there are serious doubts regarding integrity, ethics and character. Any CEO or senior management role will require the person holding that office to display an ability and willingness to raise the stakes when times are tough, and gladly assume more responsibility when called upon. Is the candidate willing and able to make hard and unpopular decisions? Will he take full responsibility for the result of such a decision? These are all examples of foundation factors: if they are not in place, the foundation is too weak to invite any further examination of other selection factors.

Obstacles

Deciding what a candidate should *not* reveal in interview sessions is essential, too. By that I mean: which obstacles might disqualify a candidate, even if they meet all the other requirements? For a leadership role or general management position, weak social skills come to mind, as do being unable to give a presentation. Or what if a candidate fits the profile of a narcissist? Someone like that is ultimately going to let his or her own interests prevail over the company's. Regardless of how talented that person might be in other respects, I believe narcissism is a fatal and disqualifying flaw. So is a lack of integrity. Despite their perfect score on all other counts, a candidate who presents any of the obstacles should be immediately disqualified from further consideration. Ideally then, you should use a feedback form with weighted criteria and an additional category of criteria weighing the obstacles. An example of such a form is provided here (with a more extensive version to be found in Appendix 2).

CANDIDATE'S NAME: DATE: INTERVIEWER:	WEIGHTING:	CANDIDATE'S SCORE:
Foundation factor Specific description of the preferences and demands regarding this selection factor	Non-negotiable	
Criterion 1 Specific description of the preferences and demands regarding this selection factor	Weighting on a scale of 1-5; with 5 being most important and 1 least important	
Criterion 2 Specific description of the preferences and demands regarding this selection factor	Weighting on a scale of 1-5; with 5 being most important and 1 least important	
Criterion 3 Specific description of the preferences and demands regarding this selection factor	Weighting on a scale of 1-5; with 5 being most important and 1 least important	
Criterion 4 Specific description of the preferences and demands regarding this selection factor	Weighting on a scale of 1-5; with 5 being most important and 1 least important	
Criterion 5 Specific description of the preferences and demands regarding this selection factor	Weighting on a scale of 1-5; with 5 being most important and 1 least important	
Criterion 6 Specific description of the preferences and demands regarding this selection factor	Weighting on a scale of 1-5; with 5 being most important and 1 least important	
Obstacles (de-selection factors) which stand in the way of fulfilling the position. Examples include: a huge ego and loner-type behaviour	Disqualifier	
Additional remarks from the interviewer:		

Core Selection Factors

John Beeson and I have both formulated a third category, the core selection factors. These are absolutely critical capacities which will finally determine who gets the job, in other words: decisive skills, personality traits and motivational needs. These are the criteria which you have drafted as the basis for the structured interview. When an executive leadership position is under consideration, the ability to assemble an effective management team of the very best people is one of the core selection factors. All CEOs or managers need to see this as a key part of their job, though in reality they often delegate this to lower management. Another core selection factor for any management role is the ability to mobilise or inspire others. The same principle applies to strategic thinking. What matters is that you not merely mention such criteria, but define what you mean by them. After all, on the job different people have various interpretations of terms like "people manager", "analytic mind" and "strategy builder".

Be specific in your expectations for these core selection factors and – equally important – be sure to rule out generic terms such as "peace broker", "team player" or "energetic manager". Otherwise you will find yourself without a clear description of what these refer to, in terms of behaviour on the job in this context.

THREE CATEGORIES FOR SELECTING TALENT

1. Foundation or non-negotiable factors: Think of the factors a candidate must have to be given serious consideration for the position. One of these is ethics; others include integrity and discernible character. For senior management roles, you could require an ability to take on extra responsibilities, or a skill for tough decision-making and the relevant sense of responsibility.

2. Obstacles: Conversely, these are criteria you do *not* want a candidate to display. They might have the foundation factors and core selection factors, possibly even an abundance of them. However, if they tick the boxes for criteria deemed to be obstacles, it is a clear no. Period. Narcissism is one such obstacle, and a tendency to always put their own interest above that of the company is another.

3. Critical or core selection factors: These are crucial criteria which a candidate must meet. A CEO, for instance, must have the ability to assemble a strong management team, be able to inspire and encourage people, or be an excellent strategist.

Despite agreeing with John Beeson that you should include a category of core selection factors my colleagues and I like to wait until a later stage to make this assessment because we find determining integrity, character and ethics beyond the feasible scope of an interview. We prefer to use other avenues for assessing these key elements. We might do an in-depth integrity check, a thorough examination of references and a canvass of the motivational needs of a candidate. By using the feedback form, we then score the other two selection factors. We always go on to estimate the obstacles which might prevent the candidate from executing the job well. In practice, combining the weighted criteria with the categories of non-negotiables, obstacles and core selection factors is a viable option too. The feedback form in Appendix 2 is a useful tool for this.

TRANSPARENT SELECTION CRITERIA

Significantly, the advantage of meticulously categorising your criteria goes beyond a simple differentiation; it compels you to check the candidates for counterproductive attributes which should preclude them from being selected for the position. In addition, you will be able to offer candidates a better explanation as to why they do not qualify for the job, something which applies to both internal candidates and ones from outside the company. This more transparent selection process avoids any charge of subjectivity or nepotism.

A third advantage of this way of working is that the selection committee and others involved in the decision are obliged to pay close attention to the non-negotiable criteria. Our office has encountered several instances of clients believing they had reached a consensus, when they turned out not to agree on various elements and in fact had divergent job descriptions in mind. When this happens, it is highly unlikely they will reach an identical judgment, and it is back to the drawing board for everyone. Sometimes a description of the criteria results in a completely new job description. I remember well the time we were approached to conduct the search for a marketing manager for an international transportation company. We discovered in working out with them the criteria for the focused interview that they were really looking for a business development manager. Every new search calls for a thorough examination to discover what is at the heart of the position, to uncover which criteria are non-negotiable, and to provide reasons for those criteria.

At first you will likely have some difficulty defining the five or six ultimate criteria for the position you wish to fill, requirements that you simply refuse to compromise on.

Devising an effective form for your feedback which includes weighted or categorised criteria, is something of a repetitive journey. Your level of understanding will grow as you become more astute at drawing up the criteria and subsequent weighting. This is a perfect match for agile ways of working: *try a lot of stuff and keep what works*. As you try a variety of things on for size, you continue to adjust your method based on your experience and the latest information.

METHOD OF "BLIND ANALYSIS"

One way to increase the agility and objectivity of your feedback form is to separate the people who devise the criteria and decide the weighting from the ones who are going to conduct the interview. Physicists call this method "blind analysis". It results in less bias and prejudice.

Selecting Agile Talent

Enough for now on how to select talent. The next step is to ensure that you can select agile talent. If you are eager to make the structured interview and the appropriate feedback form more suited to the selection of agile talent, there are at least two important steps to take. The first one is going to seem completely counterintuitive to everything you have learnt so far about how to select talent. Still, I recommend that you:

1. Do not select candidates based purely on their current abilities and knowledge, but also examine what they do not know yet. Criteria that come to mind include: having an openness to new experiences, that is, having an ability to quickly pick up unfamiliar skills – especially if the unfamiliar setting means that present skills and knowledge are of little use. Another one is the ability to add value and to hold one's own in multidisciplinary hierarchy-less teams based on an ever-evolving meritocracy.

2. Do add criteria to the feedback form which can provide an indication of how people respond to altogether different circumstances and dilemmas. Criteria that spring to mind include: intense curiosity, strength, resilience, creativity, passion, and enthusiasm.

SCORE ON A SCALE OF 1 TO 10

Asking interviewers to be concise yet detailed in their notes on the feedback form is the best way to discover why a candidate meets certain requirements. Ultimately, this should produce a final score for the position they are interviewing for. When the interviewers start to decide this score, they should of course award the most important criteria the proportionate level of importance in the number they give. The decision needs to be as realistic as possible. You should set the bar high and be wary of the tendency of many people to give average or middling scores. For decades, we have been scoring candidates on a scale of 1 to 10. You might think that different interviewers would give wildly divergent scores. In fact, an experienced group of partners and consultants at our firm seldom produces scores with a margin over 0.5 points. In fact, when the score is 8 or higher, the margin is smaller still. Therefore, the feedback form is the answer here, because its use compels you to base your decision and relevant score on those elements you have predetermined to be the most relevant. Besides, practice makes perfect when you are observing talent. If you hold several selection rounds, with different pairs of interviewers for each round, you are likely to have a solid average to show for it in the end.

"With the focused interview and its appropriate feedback form, you have a dedicated set of tools to constructively provide feedback on someone's eligibility for a position, and to make possible objective comparisons between candidates."

Setting the bar high is essential, as is reaching a consensus within the company about the minimum requirements for the job. We have been doing this for decades. Our founding partner, Johan de Vroedt, loved to say, "We are in the business of high scores, eight or nine out of ten, no meagre sixes and sevens for us." He was adamant that leniency towards a few average candidates would set off a chain reaction. The main reason was that he believed average employees are inclined to select fellow average achievers, when the time comes for them to choose new associates. This nugget of wisdom has meant that none of our interviewers would even contemplate selecting – and subsequently introducing to our clients – any candidate with a combined score below 7.5 out of ten. I recommend that you follow De Vroedt's dictum when there is a selection process underway at your company. Be bold. Let your choice be a statement. Most importantly: steer clear of the temptation to award all the candidates friendly and comfortably average scores. Giving high scores is certainly not elitist. After all, the final score is simply a reflection of how well-suited the candidate is for *this* job. Instead, they might be the perfect match for another position.

FURTHER READING

BOOKS

- John Beeson (2010). *The Unwritten Rules. The Six Skills You Need to Get Promoted to the Executive Level.* Jossey-Bass.
- Laszlo Bock (2015). *Work Rules! Insights from Inside Google That Will Transform How You Live and Lead.* Hodder & Stoughton.
- Daniel Goleman (2013). *Focus. The Hidden Driver of Excellence.* Harper Collins Publishers.
- Eric Schmidt & Jonathan Rosenberg (2014). *How Google Works.* Grand Central Publishing.

ARTICLES

- Laszlo Bock (April 7, 2015). "Here's Google's Secret to Hiring the Best People." *Wired.* Extract from his book *Work Rules!* (2015).

STAGE 2. SELECTION

Once again, I will address topics which I feel deserve more attention than they are generally given. Stage 2 deals with how to select talent. This is the stage where you use the tools and knowledge you have gathered during the prep stage. By now, you have designed a feedback form with five or six criteria that all the interviewers agree are clear and indisputable. The selection team has been assembled to include the line manager and a recruitment expert or someone from HR. One or more close colleagues are next, and possibly some subordinates. If you have opted to include the latter, you need to be sure that they are not angling for the job themselves, as this could rather cloud their objectivity. Finally, you might have taken a leaf out of Google's book and asked a staffer from a completely different field to join the selection team.

You will have devised a selection path, consisting of several rounds, with each interview being conducted by a different pair of interviewers. If they did not take notes during the conversation, they should do so directly after the structured interview. They should fill in the feedback form and score each of the candidates on a scale from 1 to 10. To prevent people influencing each other, sharing of candidate evaluations at this stage is strictly off-limits. There is a dedicated session at the end of the selection process to evaluate all the findings from the various selection tools. Next order of business: decision time.

STEP 5. SCAN THE CANDIDATE'S BACKGROUND

"If you are the smartest person in the room, you are definitely in the wrong room."

MICHAEL DELL

Interviewers everywhere are eager to form a crystal-clear picture of candidates and their personalities. Of course this is a relevant part of the process, as is taking a close look at the candidate's background. The smart thing to do is to examine:

■ The professional background of the candidate: who are the people on their team and who make up their extended professional network?

■ The personal background of the candidate

THE CANDIDATE'S PROFESSIONAL BACKGROUND

One of the best ways to separate the average from the excellent where talent is concerned is to zoom in on the people they surround themselves with. Truly outstanding leaders and managers never forget that they depend on the people around them for achieving remarkable and impressive company targets. For this reason, they tend to hire the brightest and the best they can find.

Within our firm we intentionally look beyond the individual when we are selecting talent, and we pay close attention to the people they hired in their present job. Are their immediate colleagues and subordinates able to equal or even surpass the candidate in skills and achievement? What kind of people are they in touch with, professionally? This is all highly relevant information, because you can tell a good candidate from the grade of people they select!

Someone who dedicated a large chunk of his working life to talent management and who conducted remarkable interviews was David Ogilvy, the 20th century advertising master. I am inspired by his assertion that true talent loves to gather excellent achievers around them, to fill in the gaps in their own expertise and areas of improvement – regardless of how talented they are. Here's how he put it: "First, make yourself a reputation for being a creative genius. Second, surround yourself with partners who are better than you are. Third, leave them to go get on with it." I have found this to be excellent advice, even for those of us not yet recognised for our creative genius.

To Ogilvy, the ideal corporate structure resembles Russian Matryoshka dolls, an ever-growing collection of greater people. If you are bold enough to hire those who are greater or better than you, you will end up with an organisation of giants.

Some people may react cynically to this principle, saying that there are plenty of CEOs and top managers who may be talented and yet are bent on selecting weaker individuals to work for them so that they can rule without being opposed. With very few exceptions, such managers are what I referred to earlier as Sun Kings: they prefer to surround themselves with people who might, at first glance, appear to be good at their job but who turn out to be nothing more than submissive followers and dutiful implementers, totally in the manager's power. I believe that most of the spate of recent business implosions can be attributed to this kind of CEO. Potential hires like this are to be avoided at all costs, regardless of where they might have worked previously, or how talented they are in other respects.

THE CANDIDATE'S PERSONAL BACKGROUND

Keeping one's business and personal lives separate may seem ideal, but it is fast becoming impossible to do so in a world where the different spheres of people's lives are converging more and more. For that reason it is useful to examine candidates' personal lives for the wealth of information home life can reveal about how they might go about their job. Naturally, without prior permission you cannot investigate the personal life of a candidate at random. You can however be explicit in asking personal questions during an interview, or subtly involving someone's spouse or partner in the selection process. It is essential to be sure that you are on the right side of your country's pertinent legislation and regulations. Besides, a candidate should not feel pressured into answering such questions; you must remain meticulous and transparent in your selection process, avoiding questions which are obviously disrespectful or rude.

I have often worked alongside talented and ambitious colleagues who would be drawn into something of a juggling act. Quite simply, their spouses did not fully support their careers. The reverse might also apply: I remember a candidate of average abilities who seemed to be an extraordinary networker. Apparently, he had managed to introduce countless leading business executives to each other. It turned out that his wife, a long-time diplomat, was in fact the driving force behind these introductions. After their divorce, his own network crumbled.

"I noticed that the dynamic range between what an average person could accomplish and what the best person could accomplish was 50 or 100 to 1. Given that, you're well advised to go after the cream of the cream."

STEVE JOBS

CONCLUSION

Are you determined to look at candidates from every possible angle? Then you should keep their entire background in mind: who have they surrounded themselves with, professionally and personally? Do they surround themselves with people who put up a fight for what they believe is the right course of action and offer serious feedback, or are they simply yes-men who follow orders? Worthwhile candidates know full well that a company atmosphere that encourages employees to speak up is an invigorating place to work.

> **"If each of us hires people who are smaller than we are, we shall become a company of dwarfs. But if each of us hires people who are bigger than we are, we shall become a company of giants."**
>
> DAVID OGILVY, ADVERTISING AND MARKETING MASTERMIND

FURTHER READING

BOOKS

- Bethany McLean & Peter Elkind (2004). *The Smartest Guys in the Room: The Amazing Rise and Scandalous Fall of Enron.* Portfolio Trade.
- David Ogilvy (2012). *Confessions of an Advertising Man.* Southbank Publishing.

ARTICLES

- "The 10 Worst Corporate Accounting Scandals of All Time." Infographic. http://www.accounting-degree.org/scandals/.

STEP 6. EXAMINE LEARNING AGILITY

> **"Learning agility is an important universal indication of top talent. Paired with adaptability it is one of the essential characteristics of innovative leadership and agile talent."**

As tempting as it may be to recruit someone with years of experience in a similar job, it is not the Holy Grail. Research conducted in 2014 by Claudio Fernández-Aráoz and published in the *Harvard Business Review* showed conclusively that experience, while not of trivial account, is perpetually overrated. In recent years, other key performance qualities have become popular. These include the right motivation, mental acuity, commitment, determination and openness to new things. I welcome this development, though I am convinced that selecting people based on those qualities alone is not going to cut it.

In a world in flux – the impact of which is unprecedented – positions themselves are evolving before our very eyes. An organisation has precious little use for employees with outdated knowledge. "Past performance is no guarantee of future results" applies to working as well as investing. Someone may achieve great things in one job, and still be confronted with outdated knowledge in the immediate future, which ultimately renders them obsolete.

In the very near future, it will become impossible to select people based on their current skills and experience and expect them to perform well on the job. You need to shift your focus to finding future-proof staffers. As businesses come to depend more on agile talent, their only way forward to successfully cope with the future is by unleashing their own employees. Selecting the right people then takes on monumental importance: people who are adaptable and resilient, and who can learn in completely new circumstances. Later in this chapter, we shall discover how a significant degree of introspection helps, as does a positive and constructive type of self-criticism. Often positive qualities in future-proof talent such as curiosity, resilience, adaptability and learning agility will have to be marshalled in the battle with traditional ways of doing things, disguised as "our company culture". This chapter will focus on learning ability and introspection because of their pivotal impact on agile talent's future success.

WHAT IS LEARNING AGILITY?

Learning agility is a mental trait whereby a person is willing and able to learn from new experiences and then apply this knowledge in situations that are often unforeseen and challenging. *Unlearning*, or the ability to let go of familiar opinions and ways of working, is a key dimension of learning ability.

A high score for learning agility indicates that the candidate is someone who can learn more and faster in unfamiliar situations. Such people proactively invite feedback, seek out new challenges and excel at discovering patterns within the unfamiliar.

> **"Learning agility is the capacity for rapid continuous learning from experience. It means giving up what may have worked in the past."**
>
> MONIQUE VALCOUR, *HARVARD BUSINESS REVIEW*, DECEMBER 2015

I believe that learning agility is the ultimate predictor of future success in roles of leadership and management in our new and tumultuous world. This is why executive search has begun supplementing criteria such as experience and skills with other criteria such as personality and learning agility – depending on the position and its context. The chapter dealing with step 2 provides ample opportunity to read about this.

John Sullivan, an internationally renowned Silicon Valley HR leader, says that learning agility has become the ultimate distinguishing characteristic for the rapidly-evolving business world. Laszlo Bock is of the same mind. He tells people that Google views learning agility as the leading predictor of success in the future, leaving factors like intelligence and education gasping for breath as they are left behind. It is a rare quality in candidates. Korn/Ferry Institute vice president Kenneth De Meuse estimates a mere 15 percent of employees have strongly developed learning agility. Furthermore, research by The Corporate Leadership Council suggests that no more than 30 percent of current high per-formers have the required potential to do excellent work in a higher position. It makes sense to take learning agility into account during the focused interview, in the reference checks and in the test or assessment stage, all of which make up the selection process.

WHY IS LEARNING AGILITY CRUCIALLY IMPORTANT?

There are several reasons for learning agility being more important than ever before. Here are two:

1. Rapid developments in technology make ongoing personal advancement imperative and place serious demands on learning agility. Simply because the developments never slow down, people are forced to improve themselves if they wish to keep up. The time-honoured **Peter Principle** describes how people are generally promoted to the point where they reach their own level of incompetence. A while back I amended it with what I call the Charles Principle (after Charles Darwin). The Charles Principle states that people who cannot keep developing themselves – cannot keep adapting to ever-changing demands – are now becoming incompetent *within* their current role and will lose the struggle for survival in business. Former Korn/Ferry executive Ken-neth De Meuse coined a similar aphorism, calling it the Paul Principle.

2. Globalisation requires development and learning agility, as the world is rapidly becoming increasingly interconnected, Brexit and Donald Trump notwithstanding. More businesses than ever are expanding their markets in-ternationally, often on a global scale. More information automatically means more complexity as well. Businesses are now operating in different cultures, interacting with a wider variety of foreign languages and broader ranges of legislation and trade agreements. International and cultural differences and the implications of these developments, require training on the part of man-

agers and staffers alike. Fast learners have a better chance of beating their competition, never mind keeping up with them, which is the bare minimum. In other words: the pace of learning is well on its way to overtaking knowledge itself in terms of importance.

"The Peter Principle describes how people are generally promoted to the point where they reach their own level of incompetence. Soon, this principle will be replaced by the Charles Principle. This means that people are now becoming incompetent within their current role, unless they manage to keep developing themselves."

LEARNING AGILITY IN ASSESSMENTS

One way to measure learning agility is to present candidates with completely new situations in an assessment to see how quickly they learn to cope. Using online assessments is another way. There are various tools available in this field; one of them is the model used by HFMtalentindex and Korn/Ferry. This model measures learning agility through four separate factors and one transcending element: self-awareness. This last element strongly affects the other four. They are:

1. **Change agility.** Does the candidate enjoy change? Are they interested in trying out new things? Are they curious? People with high change agility tend to be passionate about new experiences, and are keen to explore the unknown.

2. **Results agility.** Is the candidate able to achieve goals in circumstances that may seem strange, unfamiliar and challenging? People with high results agility are generally focused on and driven by a need to achieve. Often confident and ambitious, they are never unfazed by stressful situations.

3. **People agility.** Is the candidate able to deal with a variety of people? Those with high people agility have an open mind to others with different opinions

and from different backgrounds. They are eager to gain in-depth knowledge of others, and can easily adapt to different surroundings or cultures.

4. **Mental agility.** Is the candidate someone who can find original or unique ways to solve a problem? People with high mental agility are frequently provoked by new ideas, relishing the opportunity to think outside the box. They are more adept at discerning patterns in new circumstances than others are.

5. **Self-awareness.** Does the candidate have a clear and realistic view of his strengths, weaknesses and areas needing improvement? People with a high level of self-awareness have a remarkably acute sense of their own strengths and weaknesses. They are drawn to self-improvement and are eager to deepen their understanding of themselves and the world around them. A high level of self-awareness can work as leverage for the other aspects of learning agility. Conversely, a low level might have the opposite effect. Evidently, someone who never misses an opportunity to improve their weak areas will be more effective at learning than someone who feels they are already perfect.

CHECKING LEARNING AGILITY DURING INTERVIEWS

The best way to measure learning agility may be the use of a dedicated assessment tool. However, you can perform an initial check of agility during the interview. At the very least, I suggest you do these five things:

1. **Scan the resume for learning agility indicators.** Candidates with a high learning agility often illustrate their resume with examples proving they can learn easily. They might give straightforward mentions of challenging projects they completed which pushed them beyond their comfort zone. They have no trouble explaining what they learnt from them. Next, you need to verify these mentions on the resume, and check if the candidate's self-professed strong learning agility and eagerness to scale a steep learning curve are indeed accurate.

Marcel Levi is an internist as well as the CEO of the prestigious University College London Hospitals. He once described to me how his mentor, Professor Jan Wouter ten Cate, relished purposely catching him off-guard by handing him large projects and responsibilities. Once, Ten Cate was due to give a lecture in Copenhagen for a group of renowned medical experts, yet he suddenly decided Levi should do it instead. For two weeks, Levi lost sleep over this, but he managed to give the lecture anyway and found it a huge learning experience. Ten Cate was an ideal mentor, pushing the young doctor to deepen h s knowledge about subjects that Levi found to be less interesting such as statistics and epidemiology, and to broaden his horizons by attending Oxford University to study microbiology for a year, an experience he still treasures. Despite his determination to be a doctor, as a teenager Levi took a vocational course in catering! When he looks back at his varied career, Levi can tell you exactly why he found certain activities challenging and highly instructive at the same time. For many years, Levi managed to juggle more than a handful of activities: teaching, working part-time in internal medicine, managing a university hospital and being a CEO. He relates to his patients effortlessly, speaking with them on equal terms. In his work as hospital executive, he can easily discuss a wide range of topics with his medical peers.

2. **Pose a question on "ranking".** Have the candidate rank the five or six criteria you deem essential for the job. Evaluate this candidate's responses against those of other applicants. (All candidates should list their strongest characteristics first. What is their greatest strength and how will the company reap the most benefit from it if they were hired? It might be conceptual thinking, strong implementing skills, being a good manager of people, making stakeholders feel included, practicing agile learning, or possessing a wealth of experience in the field.) Should the first three qualities the candidate lists not include anything indicating agile learning capacities, you need to direct the oblivious aspirant towards a deeper discussion of this topic. If you still cannot discern any demonstrable learning agility on the part of the candidate, nor ability for personal reinvention, you should certainly subtract some points from that person's total score.

3. **Pose a question on learning objectives.** Ask candidates what they think their main learning objectives will be in their possible new role. What do they plan to learn in the first 100 days, and over the first six months? Being able to correctly determine learning objectives is not all that matters here. The best people will have already begun to imagine what their role will entail, and how they need to adopt relevant new skills. A conscious effort on their part, backed up with a detailed and factual plan to achieve their objectives, is one of the first indications of their learning agility.
4. **Pose a question on interview prep.** I have often noticed that candidates with remarkable learning agility often have unorthodox ways of preparing for the interview. Without exception, they have gone beyond a perfunctory search on Google or the obligatory once-over of the corporate website. So when you find out what they know about the organisation, you need to be sure to ask the candidates where they found their information. People with strong learning agility capacities have usually done more extensive research. They have examined verifiable sources of information and can produce less obvious facts by, for example, chatting with former top executives or other stakeholders who recently left the company. This way they can display inside knowledge about the organisation that will score points with interviewers.
5. **Present the candidate with a case study of an unfamiliar field.** Another way to elicit a first impression of candidates' learning agility is to present them with a case study of an area they are unfamiliar with. I prefer to offer such case study complete with dilemmas, at our offices. Why? Because otherwise you may end up with an assessment of the learning agility of people entirely different from the candidates': their helpful friends!

Given the increased significance of learning agility, I strongly encourage all our clients to include it in every structured interview, and make it into a separate entry on the feedback form.

INTROSPECTION

In my opinion, introspection merits separate attention. In all my interviews, I spend a disproportionate amount of time on it, and I highly recommend that you include it in your search for agile talent.

"We have found that learning ability is the leading predictor of success – no. 1 above intelligence and education."

LASZLO BOCK, FORMER SENIOR VICE PRESIDENT HR AT GOOGLE

CEOs who recognise the significance of introspection are no longer a lonely minority. Take the CEO of DSM, a Netherlands-based global Life Sciences and Materials Sciences company active in health, nutrition and materials. Feike Sijbesma shared an interesting fact with me during an interview: every single one of the talented individuals in DSM's high potential pool must possess this indispensable quality. If they cannot accept their assessments turning up several serious areas of improvement, they are not allowed onto the management development path. "Whenever someone trivialises the weak points or areas of focus which were unearthed in an assessment or 360-degree feedback review, I see this as a red flag," explains Sijbesma. "Any truly great leader will have a strong introspective tendency, always open to constructive criticism and scrutiny of areas needing improvement. Great leaders never stop learning new skills, and they are acutely aware of their own insecurities and doubts."

This description by the DSM executive rings true for me, as it matches my own experience. The very best candidates come prepared with a list of their greatest strengths, including substantial proof of their achievements. Additionally, they can describe the moments throughout their career when they learnt the most, and they can articulate how their unique blend of interests and activities helped them land an important promotion. Active introspection – a firmly held belief that there is room for improvement in everyone – is second nature to them. Their self-confidence relative to their strengths is precisely what helps them admit freely what skills and characteristics they lack.

AUTOMATIC AND REAL-TIME FEEDBACK

One useful method to cultivate your introspection is to proactively invite feedback. Those with high learning agility are often already inclined to do so. Traditional methods to do this are effective, to be sure, though there are automatic feedback mechanisms now, too.

TruQu for instance, is an organisation which produces feedback software and a dedicated feedback-app. These products enable employees within organisations to ask for feedback continually, and give it too. Thanks to TruQu, people now have the opportunity to keep on learning and developing themselves, through gathering and giving feedback informally. This feedback might come from a colleague, their manager or a client. Additionally, you can give people compliments through the app. It is a way to enhance commitment and participation. Staffers are matched to each other based on mutually complementary skills and characteristics through the software. Person A might be paired with person B because one of them has better skills in a particular area. This means people are given feedback by others they might actually learn from. This can be a huge boost to the adaptability and learning agility within an organisation. After all, a culture of healthy feedback can help employees improve their future performance simply by helping each other.

CONCLUSION

Not only is introspection essential to personal development, it is also a prerequisite for modern leadership. Without self-awareness, you cannot be a successful manager of others. Frequent introspection is the best way to further your self-awareness and find increased clarity regarding your strengths and weaknesses. The reverse of this – to be blind to one's own blind spots – can lead to monumental failure.

Longing to improve your introspection implies needing to frequently take stock of your progress and what you have learnt on the way. Did things turn out differently than you had expected? How might you achieve better results next time, using what you learnt now? Do other people agree with your self-assessment?

Of course, there are traditional methods to deepen your self-awareness – simply asking people for feedback goes back millennia. Or you might use the latest IT solutions, which allow you to receive real-time feedback from people who can, undeniably, teach you something about yourself you could not perceive easily "from the inside."

FURTHER READING

BOOKS

- Linda S. Gravett & Sheri A. Caldwell (2016). *Learning Agility. The Impact on Recruitment and Retention*. Palgrave Macmillan.
- George Hallenbeck (2016). *Learning Agility. Unlock the Lessons of Experience*. Center for Creative Leadership.

ARTICLES

- Kenneth P. De Meuse (2011). *What's Smarter Than IQ? Learning Agility. It's No.1 – Above Intelligence and Education – in Predicting Leadership Success*. The Korn Ferry Institute.
- Kenneth P. De Meuse, Guangrong Dai & George S. Hallenbeck (2010). "Learning Agility: A Construct Whose Time Has Come." *Consulting Psychology Journal: Practice and Research*, vol. 62, no. 2, pp. 119-130.
- Claudio Fernández-Aráoz (June 2014). "How to Spot Talent (Hint: Talent is Overrated)," *Harvard Business Review*.
- J.P. Flaum & Becky Winkler (June 8, 2015). "Improve Your Ability to Learn." *Harvard Business Review*.
- Koen Hofkes & Vittorio Busato (2015). *Learning Agility*. Whitepaper. HFMtalentindex.
- Douglas LaBier (August 17, 2013). "Why Business Leaders Need to Build Greater Self-Awareness." PsychologyToday.com.
- Jean Martin & Conrad Schmidt (May 2010) "How to Keep Your Top Talent." *Harvard Business Review*.
- Adam Mitchinson & Robert Morris (2014). *Learning About Learning Agility*. Whitepaper. Center for Creative Leadership.
- Patricia Steiner (August 2014). "The Impact of the Self-Awareness Process on Learning and Leading." *New England Journal of Higher Education*.
- Monique Valcour (December 31, 2015). "4 Ways to Become a Better Learner." *Harvard Business Review*.

STEP 7. LEAVE THE COMFORT ZONE – THE MAGIC OF THE UNEXPECTED

"Staying within your comfort zone is a good way to prepare for today, but it's a terrible way to prepare for tomorrow."

DAVID PETERSON, DIRECTOR OF EXECUTIVE
COACHING & LEADERSHIP AT GOOGLE

Over the course of their career, highly experienced executives will have been interviewed time and again. They know the drill and allow plenty of time to prepare for the meeting. After effortlessly explaining their strengths, they usually feel sufficiently comfortable to talk candidly about their capabilities that could stand improvement. This is fine as far as it goes, though it does mean they have had ample opportunity to think this over. However, if you are a potential employer you are really interested in exploring the imponderables – how, for example, would they react to a situation they had not previously dealt with which is beyond their control? What happens when they face opposition?

A certain type of person tends to give evasive answers when asked about weaknesses that need improvement. Even when pressured, they cannot resist offering up "humble-brag" characteristics that are not really weaknesses: for example, the GM of a company admitting he's a tad impatient waiting for his employees to produce results. Or a turnaround manager who

confesses that empathy is not his strong suit: if he is applying
to a company where drastic measures have to be taken, he may
be calculating that this "weakness" will be looked on favourably.
You should not allow yourself to be taken in by humble-brag-
garts; it is especially important to push this type of candidate
out of their comfort zone and urge them to be candid about real
areas needing improvement.

UNEXPECTED QUESTIONS WORKING THEIR MAGIC

Popular convention holds that interviews are little more than beauty contests
where aspiring hires try to show off their best profiles. This is certainly true if
careless or manipulated interviewers do little better than engage in friendly
conversations. But if candidates are not nudged out of their comfort zone
during this crucial stage of the hiring process, the company is left in the dark
about their ability to respond to the severe stress of the unexpected.

This is where the magic of the unexpected question comes to the rescue. You
simply ask the candidate something they could not possibly have prepared for,
or present them with a case study they have never seen before. Then, sit back
and watch their response unfold.

All sorts of questions spring to mind. In my personal experience, the best
time for the unexpected question is at the end of the interview. Just wait for
the candidate to feel completely relaxed, starting to exhale with relief, and
then hit them with an unforeseen question.

One of my former clients told me about a recent incident where this happened. Prior to working as vice president of Procurement, he was a partner
at McKinsey & Company. There, he had interviewed a candidate who was well
aware of the partners' interest in number crunching and their penchant for
conceptual thinking. The interview went swimmingly, its atmosphere laidback
and the conversation ebullient as the two men chatted about mutual friends
and shared interests – they had played for the same hockey club, and their
wives had been members of the same sorority. After spending a pleasant hour
together, my client casually changed the subject, saying that he had "just one

last question". He paused for breath, poured some more coffee for everyone and passed a plate of biscuits to the candidate. "How many ping pong balls do you think might fit in one of those new Boeing 787 Dreamliners?"

My client was not particularly interested in the mathematical accuracy of the answer. Instead, he was eager to hear what approach the candidate would take, and significantly, how he would react to this sudden and unorthodox question. Would he manage to stay calm and collected to a question lobbed out of left field for which he could not game plan? How well would he cope with an unexpected dilemma?

Laszlo Bock does not approve of this kind of question. He believes – and rightly so – that these questions have little predictive validity of someone's future job performance. However, they can supply you with valuable information on how someone copes under pressure, particularly when confronted with the unexpected. The non-negotiable factors from the focused interview, in addition to the other selection tools, will provide information about how a candidate might fulfil their new role, and the unexpected question can show you a glimpse of their personality. For this reason, I would suggest that you use them both.

How many ping pong balls can you fit into a Boeing 787 Dreamliner?

Variations on this theme are abundant. One of the founding partners of our office, Johan de Vroedt, was a firm believer in this method. An accomplished interviewer, he would come up with the most bizarre question you could imagine. Besides, he enjoyed creating offbeat situations during an interview. I remember the trick he played on me when I first met him. I was there to interview for a position as Managing Director of the Dutch national Social Services/Job Centre, and he was one of two interviewers. During the session we discussed various questions pertaining to my ambitions, work experience and personal development.

Suddenly, the phone rang in the conference room where we were seated. One of the interviewers answered the call, which turned out to be from a celebrity acquaintance of his. Despite such a significant person making the call, I assumed it would be a brief conversation – this was hardly a convenient time for a chat. I could not have been more wrong. "What a wonderful surprise, it's great to hear from you," began what turned out to be a private conversation that seemed to go on forever. Though he did discreetly turn away from me as he spoke, their conversation was about private matters – recent holidays, a visit to a museum and the like.

At first, I felt extremely uncomfortable being made a witness to this phone call, and I sat there wondering how I should be reacting to what was happening. After a while, though, I started to relax. Though far from feeling in charge of the situation, I managed to achieve some sort of calm. Smiling faintly, I glanced at the two men on the opposite side of the table and leaned back in my chair.

Inadvertently, I had stumbled on the correct response, for the phone conversation was suddenly cut short – "I'll have to call you back later." Afterwards, one of the interviewers told me that "we do more than simply look for the right answers; we want to make our decision based on your response to anything out of the ordinary." (Full disclosure – eventually we reached the joint decision that I was not suited for this job, after having worked in a far more competitive English environment for years. But apart from meeting Johan de Vroedt, I learned a valuable interviewing strategy from this interview; ever since, I have made it a point to always include an unexpected question or an unforeseen situation.)

WHAT DOES THE PARTNER THINK?

One of my favourite tactics is to find out what a candidate's partner would describe as their spouse's most remarkable personality trait. At the end of an interview covering a wide range of topics, I enjoy asking someone what they believe their spouse would say, if they were asked about the candidate. What would the person they share their life with, the person who knows them best, have to say about the candidate's talents? Which characteristics does the partner find annoying beyond endurance? I find it fascinating that many candidates, who have been married for decades, draw a blank when you ask them how their spouse would respond to: "What quality makes you unique and extraordinary – out of all your different qualities, that is? And what do they find the most annoying thing about you?" Interestingly, they usually give a different answer than when you ask them what they themselves think they excel at. Of course, there is no single perfect answer to this question. But it's indicative of *something* when a candidate has no idea what their spouse thinks. Are they just not communicating, is the candidate interested in the spouse's opinion, does the prospective hire tend to ventilate their own opinions without ever listening to others? Does someone who has little or no interest in what other people have to say even qualify as a leader? Naturally, you should not consider the answer to this question in isolation. It should, however, be considered together with all the other selection tools you have used.

"What would your spouse say is the quality that makes you unique and extraordinary – out of all your different qualities, that is? And what do they find most annoying about you?"

CONCLUSION

A traditional part of the screening process is to probe candidates for their strong points and weaknesses, a ritual senior job aspirants expect. But a smart future employer wants more than rehearsed responses to standard questions. The employer wants to know how the prospective executive responds to on-job pressures, unforeseen dilemmas, and setbacks. Asking an unexpected question or creating an unorthodox situation in the interview are two ways to find out. Nowadays interviewers often borrow a technique from psychological researchers and include an impossible assignment or question which no one could possibly complete in a set amount of time. The goal here is to monitor how candidates react to being forced to abandon their comfort zone.

FURTHER READING

BOOKS

- William Poundstone (2012). *Are You Smart Enough to Work at Google? Trick Questions, Zen-like Riddles, Insanely Difficult Puzzles, and Other Devious Interviewing Techniques You Need to Know to Get a Job Anywhere in the New Economy.* Little, Brown and Company.

ARTICLES

- Glassdoor (March 28, 2016). "Top 10 Oddball Interview Questions for 2016." www.glassdoor.com.

STAGE 3. VERIFICATION

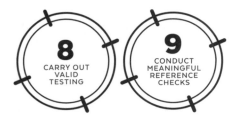

The first objective of this book is to discuss agile talent itself, not necessarily selection methods which discern agility. Still, I am convinced that if you add some agility to your selection process, the odds of it yielding future-proof talent will increase. A key part of the agile way of working is verifying your preliminary findings. This section of the book examines two ways to do this: testing candidates and effectively checking references.

STEP 8.
VALID TESTS

"Often, the amount of time spent on selecting and testing candidates is inversely proportionate to the gravity of the position."

FRANK VAN LUIJK, ASSESSMENT PSYCHOLOGIST

AND EXPERT ON LEADERSHIP

While testing candidates for executive positions may not be common practice, I believe it is important to do so. Otherwise, you might be tempted to base your decision upon one single method of selection such as the structured interview. Still, many organisations are reluctant to apply tests as part of their selection. Of numerous possible reasons, the most prevalent are:

1. Reliable tests do not come cheap

2. People are inclined to question the predictive validity of tests

Any good candidate will have a superior resume, all the right qualifications and most importantly, a sterling career track record. All this does not provide the full picture, though. We have already discussed how a new job context might be the reason that a formerly excellent executive fails to achieve the results everyone had hoped for. Conversely, a manager or staffer might have enormous untapped potential that does not stand out in their resume because their last job did not make any demands of a particular skill. Their talent has not had the opportunity to realise its full promise.

IQ, certain skills and knowledge are all elements which are easily laid bare in an interview or by means of other "traditional" selection methods. Personality traits and motivations can prove more difficult to recognise – particularly motivational needs. They have an enormous impact on how we act and yet they cannot be detected through straightforward observation. For this reason, it is critical to use tests to determine what they are.

TO TEST OR NOT TO TEST?

Deciding to have a candidate tested is the best way to discover those elements which prove difficult to uncover using traditional methods. You need to ascertain that the test meets these conditions:

1. It must be reliable.
2. It must be valid.
3. It must be predictive.
4. Furthermore, you have to know what exactly the test measures, and how easily test outcomes can be skewed by someone.

In addition to these prerequisites, it is vital that the test be conducted accurately. Having an objective scoring system is important, as is a concise, logical manual to work with. When you embark on the process of choosing a test with which to verify your review of the candidate, I would encourage you to take the aforementioned conditions into account. The following is a more comprehensive look at these conditions.

1. Reliability

Psychologists refer to a test as reliable when it produces stable and consistent results under the same conditions. A common measure in the academic world is to test a group of people twice over a period of time to see how consistent the test results are. This is called test-retest reliability.

This is not as straightforward as you might think, particularly with respect to tests of personality and someone's motivational needs.

Even if a test produces virtually identical results, it does not necessarily mean that its results are accurate or possesses serious predictive validity.

2. Validity

Whenever we feel confident of a test being valid, we are referring to the use of certain paradigms in that particular test. For instance, do the questions provide substantial information on the element you wish to measure? Assessing the validity of a test compels you to review whether it is measuring the element you are interested in.

3. Predictive Validity

Another key element to consider before choosing a test is its predictive validity. What does the outcome of the test mean regarding how successful someone will be in a certain position or work situation? The only way to determine whether a test is of practical value is to decide whether it is both reliable and valid.

Prediction is a murky area. There are tests which are highly reliable, but in practice show poor predictive validity. Even though they are consistent in producing identical results, they end up giving you scant information on the very thing you had meant to test. There is little merit in having a candidate tested if the test offers low predictive validity.

4. What is Being Measured?

Sometimes, tests are popular because candidates believe the results provide accurate representations of themselves. What the test has measured, then, is in fact the self-perception of the candidate, who will have answered the questions based on how they see themselves, and – hey presto! – the test matches that perception. This does not necessarily mean the test has produced an accurate picture of the candidate. Checking whether people around the candidate can vouch for that picture is the answer to this dilemma. Should that check produce a completely different image, then you might want to consider using another test. Some testing methods are very easy to read, instantly comprehensible and are open to any interested observer swiftly figuring out how they work. While being easy to understand is a valuable feature of any testing method, the downside is that clever candidates can manage to slightly influence the outcome of such tests. The test might provide you with an idea of their IQ, but leave you empty-handed in other respects: a true picture of other elements you had meant to test.

A CONVOLUTED SUBJECT

The sheer number of tests is staggering. A fair proportion of them do the job well, though they are hard to grasp. Often jam-packed with specialist jargon, they are beyond the comprehension of laymen. Other tests might be adequate too, but require a psychologist or similar professional to administer them. Frankly, I do not think you should try to administer tests unless you have this background. Perfectly executing tests, reliable tests, requires the special training and skills of a professional. At our firm, we consistently and carefully select outside experts to carry out all our tests.

PRACTICAL CONSIDERATIONS

Over the course of the selection process, candidates will be tested on many different things. However, this does not seem to apply to top executive positions. In my work in search and recruitment, I have often seen managers run the gauntlet to determine their eligibility for a new position. Assessments, questionnaires, personality tests, they are subjected to every evaluation contrivance. However, when we (to mix metaphors) move up the pyramid to CEOs and (supervisory) board members, testing suddenly becomes far less prevalent. Experienced candidates are wont to remark, "Oh, but I have been tested plenty of times already." This is plainly true, and the hiring organisation will often decide to back down and forget about testing altogether. The problem is that previous tests offer only sparse information on how well a candidate might fare in this new position, in an unfamiliar context. Besides, managers may just have undergone various tests for IQ, skills and personality. Tests for motivational needs are far less common. Testing supervisory board members – who often had illustrious careers as CEOs – is generally regarded as not done. How could you possibly consider submitting such a distinguished individual to something as *infra dig* as a test?

In short, CEOs and supervisory board members often end up being tested far less extensively, having far less scrutiny heaped upon them, than the managers who report to them do. When you consider how the cost of a failed selection match tends to increase in proportion to the gravity of a position, it will be evident how unwise this truly is.

For years, it was the custom to only submit the preferred candidate to tests or assessments at the end of the selection process. Things are starting to change, though. Tech businesses and people involved in the selection of IT managers have become more inclined to have candidates submit to tests at an earlier stage of selection. Often, all candidates end up being tested and the test itself determines who is invited for the actual selection interview. In the past, assessments could only be conducted at a dedicated assessment centre, whereas now they can often be done online, saving time and money. You can see the implications for assessing larger groups of people prior to the interview stage.

SEVERAL TESTS OF MOTIVATIONAL NEEDS

While testing IQ, skills and personality traits has become fairly mainstream, exploring the primary social needs of a candidate is far less so. I believe it is a mistake to leave this exploration aside; after all, this part of a test will focus on how someone is inclined to behave most of the time.

Personality tests are widely accepted by experts – the Big Five test above all. Tests with the objective of unravelling a person's motivational needs are somewhat more controversial.

I have had good results with the TAT, or Thematic Apperception Test. It is a projective test, first developed by Christiana Morgan and Henry Murray, and expanded on by David McClelland. Most tests of social drives or needs tend to raise a lot of critical questions. The TAT is no different. The key point of contention: the test's validity.* Tests based on psychometrics, developed later than the TAT, faced similar objections. You should know that no single test can produce perfect results.

Thematic Apperception Test (TAT)

The TAT consists of a series of drawings or photos. Candidates are then asked to write down a narrative which encompasses the time leading up to the situation depicted, the situation itself and whatever happens next. The images and people are purposely open to multiple interpretations. For example: two people pictured talking to each other could be either arguing or having a spirited, friendly discussion. A candidate's interpretation is indicative of their way of thinking, that is the idea behind this test. Over the course of the test being administered, this technique is repeated several times by presenting the candidate with different situations. A specially trained expert can then apply a strict protocol to interpret which primary needs are dominant in that candidate. The unique blend of these needs – the orientation – has already been covered extensively in the chapter on step 2. In a nutshell: the candidate is given scores from 1-100 relating to the three primary social needs (achievement, affiliation and power).

The underlying principle of the TAT is that people tend to project their own motives, concealed needs, fears and expectations onto the narrative they describe. Images open to varied interpretations will then be represented according to their own unconscious imaginings and experiences. In fact, they will project their interior world onto the reality outside themselves. The narrative someone writes down thus becomes a reflection of who they are and what motivates them.

> ## "It's critical to note that it's more important to choose the right assessors than to focus on the assessment technique."
>
> FERNÁNDEZ-ARÁOZ, GROYSBERG & NOHRIA,
> *HARVARD BUSINESS REVIEW*, WINTER 2012

The initial designers of the test believe that it can account for up to 70 to 75 percent of a person's behaviour. What the test is designed to reveal is the *reason* behind an individual's actions. People might be participating in the same activity, but displaying completely divergent behaviours. (Think back to the examples of mountain climbing or playing golf in the chapter on this step.) The TAT may be a scientifically validated test geared at exploring primary social needs, but it cannot provide a watertight 100 percent prediction of future behaviour. Still, using this test will bring depth and richness to your perception of the candidate – more than cognitive tests could do. Besides, testing tools like these are never meant to fully predict someone's behaviour, they are food for thought and conversation. By discussing their very own talents and pitfalls, a candidate can give you an idea of their introspection and you can then assess it simultaneously. The interesting thing about the TAT is that a candidate can only predict their results if they have studied this topic extensively. It is in fact nearly impossible to influence the outcome of the test. In addition to measuring self-awareness, it does a check of a person's true motivational needs. I have experienced first-hand, after making this test, that there is always a hint of inconsistency between your own perception of yourself and your identity. It can then be useful to learn more about this inconsistency. Even though mo-

---

* Dutch scientist Ber Damen studied this for his dissertation *Leadership and Motivation*, and produced several preconditions which refuted these objections.

tivational needs have fully developed by the time you are an adult, it cannot hurt to deepen your knowledge of your behaviour. It can help to avoid certain familiar personal pitfalls.

The TAT has a sound theoretical basis in the work of Harvard University's Henry Murray and Christiana D. Morgan, who developed the test, and in that of John Atkinson and David McClelland, who developed the scoring system. Provided two conditions are met, the TAT is in fact capable of producing clear indications of how a candidate will behave. First, a robust method of scoring the test should be used, for instance the one devised by David Winter. Next, it is imperative that an experienced and qualified expert be the person who administers the test and interprets its outcome.

For the TAT this would involve codifying and interpreting the narrative written by the candidate. This all happens within strictly defined parameters. In fact, studies suggest that the process of interpretation is even more important than the quality of the test itself. *Leadership and Motivation,* the dissertation by Dutch scientist Ber Damen, describes how – provided strict conditions are adhered to – the TAT can yield valuable information on needs and slightly subdue voices of criticism regarding its validity and reliability. The essential recommendation here is that the test be interpreted by properly trained experts, working according to scientific methods of collection.

Needs Assessment Questionnaire

An alternative method of identifying motivational or primary social needs is the Needs Assessment Questionnaire designed by Jan Morsch, a researcher and lecturer for the Center for Leadership and Management Development at Nyenrode Business University, the Netherlands. Despite its relative novelty, this test can assess a person's intrinsic *and* extrinsic needs, with little doubt regarding the validity and reliability of the test. Morsch has determined eight separate needs, instead of the familiar three used by McClelland.

Manifest needs	Description
The intrinsic need for achievement	A need to achieve for the person's own sake
The extrinsic need for achievement	A need to achieve to gain approval from others
The need for cooperation	A need to work with other people
The need for social interaction	A need to interact with others and strike up relationships
The need for informal power	A need to wield influence and thus impact others
The need for leadership	A need for a formal position of power
The need for independence	A need for working alone and being independent
The need for responsibility	A need to be responsible for their own work

MORSCH'S EIGHT SEPARATE NEEDS

CONCLUSION

After setting up a proper framework for the selection process, and meticulously applying the various steps from stage 2, you should make a multi-perspective decision. Do not base your verdict on one single method of selection, instead be ready to scrutinise your findings. There is not much point in conducting an assessment if it does not meet the key requirements we discussed earlier in this chapter. The match ultimately depends on the context, which is why even highly experienced senior candidates need to be properly tested and assessed. To be more specific, a test of needs and personality traits can give a good indication of future behaviour. Profiling someone's personality and motivational needs is one of the best ways to determine whether they can achieve excellence. Interviews may give you an indication of the candidate's primary social needs. However, it is sensible to make use of a dedicated test or assessment if you want to find a reliable and detailed description of their needs. After all, few people have indiscriminately high scores on just the one need; most of us have a blend of several primary needs. Only an expert can properly determine and describe this blend, otherwise you might end up with an unreliable test result. For this very reason, I always have outside consultants conduct this kind of test. You should remember though, that no single test of needs or personality can offer you a 100 percent view of a person's drives and traits. In other words, regarding these tests as absolute truth would be unwise. You are better off taking a composite view of all the different elements in the selection process.

FURTHER READING

BOOKS

- J.W. Atkinson (1992). "Motivational Determinants of Thematic Apperception." In: C.P. Smith (ed.), *Motivation and Personality. Handbook of Thematic Content Analysis*. Cambridge University Press.
- Tina Lewis Rowe (2013). *A Preparation Guide for the Assessment Center Method*. 2nd Edition. Charles C. Thomas Pub Ltd.
- Susana Urbina (2014). *Essentials of Psychological Testing (Essentials of Behavioral Science)*. 2nd Edition. Wiley.

ARTICLES

- Claudio Fernández-Aráoz, Boris Groysberg & Nitin Nohria (winter 2012). "The Definitive Guide to Recruiting in Good Times and Bad." *Harvard Business Review OnPoint*.
- F.L. Schmidt & J.E. Hunter (1998). "The Validity and Utility of Selection Methods in Personnel Psychology. Practical and Theoretical Implications of 85 Years of Research Findings." *Psychological Bulletin*, 124, pp. 262-274.
- W.D. Spangler (1992). "Validity of Questionnaire and TAT Measures of Need for Achievement. Two Meta-Analyses." *Psychological Bulletin*, 112, pp. 140-154.
- David G. Winter (1994). "Manual for Scoring Motive Imagery in Running Text." University of Michigan.

STEP 9. MEANINGFUL REFERENCE CHECKS

> **"A sign of a good leader is not how many followers you have, but how many leaders you create."**
>
> GANDHI

Throughout my career, I have counselled many clients on making changes within management and I have carried out preliminary screenings on countless candidates. Guiding clients through the selection process is an aspect of my work that I most enjoy. The vast majority of my clients realise how important it is to find the right person for the job – janitor or CEO – and are motivated and serious about selecting talent. They are well aware of the elements that a proper process ought to consist of, and how to avoid mistakes. However, the final stages of the selection process are often too condensed, leading to avoidable errors.

Here's what often happens: as the end of the selection process draws near, people start to reach a consensus about the candidate. That is when they decide to quickly check over some references, a task often delegated to associates who were neither involved in the interviewing stage of selection, nor have any knowledge of the specifics of the search. Afterwards, when things veer off course and the candidate fails to live up to expectations, people start wondering why there were no in-depth reference checks of the candidate's former employers.

AN EXCEPTIONAL SELECTION TOOL

Many people are distinctly unimpressed by the information potential and predictive validity that references might provide. They may believe that the research substantiates their opinion: after all, Frank Schmidt and John Hunter's meta-research in 1998 – widely regarded as one of the leading studies on selection tools – proved that the average predictive validity of reference checks was significantly lower than the structured interview.

I am convinced, however, that the main reason for this is the sloppy way that reference checks are carried out, limiting what in fact is a very important tool. If you follow the steps which I shall describe in this chapter, your meaningful reference checks will become a valuable signpost on the road to fewer mismatches. Appendix 1 highlights the key findings of Schmidt & Hunter's study. It shows you the average predictive validity of each selection tool. Percentages are supplied to underscore the added value of any given tool. Schmidt and Hunter recommend that you combine several selection tools – that is the underlying premise of this book as well. If you carry out the nine selection steps outlined in this book and keep in mind the importance of reference checks, I promise you that your predictive validity – your ability to pick the right person for the job – will increase dramatically.

At the top end of the market, candidates tend to be immensely capable of presenting themselves well. They have no trouble at all sharing with the interviewers what their greatest added value is – they may even radiate such an aura of capability mixed with charm that they can tell the bedazzled interviewers there might be reasons *not* to hire them! To mitigate the charisma-blinding factor it makes sense to be fastidious in your review of the observations during interviews.

How do you move to turn reference checks into a valuable tool, what aspects come into play and which elements – at the least – should you be sure to go over with a fine-toothed comb? In the pages that follow we'll focus on these four:

1. How many references? Whom do you check?
2. How do you go about making these checks?
3. To whom do you delegate the actual checking process?
4. Which questions do you need to ask (minimum list)?

HOW MANY REFERENCES AND FROM WHOM?

From time immemorial, it seems the decree has gone out: a candidate needs two reference checks. And then time being limited, the Law of Two gets whittled down to one being checked (maybe). Ideally though, the same principle should apply in talent selection as in Dutch criminal law: a single witness is as good as no witness at all!

It is my strong recommendation that you obtain references from not just two, but from at least three or four individuals. They should preferably be people from differing levels of the candidate's company. When you are recruiting a business unit manager, you might go to the CEO for information, to a close colleague, plus to someone on the team reporting to the candidate. An ideal fourth reference might be a client. This "360-degree feedback" reference check will offer you a multidimensional view of the candidate, increasing the odds of an objective picture, covering a range of the candidate's features. Their former boss can most likely give you an insight into their need for achievement, or strategic ability. Close colleagues can provide information on how cooperative the candidate is, their influence they wield; the subordinates from the candidate's team will have a clear idea of their ability to lead. Whenever a candidate proves unable to give you three or four professional references, you should immediately ask them to give a plausible reason. Any candidate with ten to fifteen years' professional experience should have no trouble providing such references. If they cannot, be very wary.

"The same principle endorsed in Dutch criminal law should apply to talent selection: a single witness is just as good as no witness at all! I recommend obtaining at least three or four references, making sure they are people from different levels of the company. Try to include at least one client. Conduct your interviews face to face."

Be Sure to Check Mutual Acquaintances

The Achilles' heel of reference checks is a mediocre execution by the person who does the check. Have you made certain that they are neutral and objective, that they are not somehow acquainted with – or even friends of – the candidate? This may seem obvious and yet it is easily overlooked. If you have even the slightest hint that the candidate and recruiter are acquainted, the necessity of checking multiple references increases drastically. In this case, you would be wise to tap into several acquaintances of both the referee and the candidate.

In the old days, you would be hard-pressed to work out who these mutual acquaintances might be, but now we have social media at our fingertips. LinkedIn and Facebook will instantly show you shared connections. Someone who is on speaking terms with the recruiter is highly unlikely to paint too rosy a picture of the candidate; after all, they will probably cross paths again in the future. There are very few people who relish the idea of having a chance remark about a candidate blow up in their face, when the reference they provided turns out to be inaccurate. It is, however, key that the referee have a clear understanding of the qualifications and characteristics which the new position requires. A close acquaintance may be perfectly willing to speak warmly of the candidate's personality, yet have insufficient knowledge of their strategic ability. Or he might be the manager of the candidate, who has had not needed to devise strategy in his current position, because they are both employed by an American multinational – the head office thinks up strategy and the national offices simply carry it out. So the manager can only speak to the executive skills of the candidate, not realising that he might in fact be a brilliant strategist.

Carte Blanche?

Being given carte blanche by the candidate to speak with whomever you wish is even better than speaking with referees who are mutual acquaintances. This is a clear show of self-confidence on their part and the first signal that you are dealing with someone who has no secrets. What you must keep in mind is that a candidate is giving you this freedom on the proviso that you proceed professionally and with integrity. I have further made it a habit to agree ahead of time that the candidate will be allowed to refute any negative references that might ensue from this free rein.

HOW TO CHECK REFERENCES

The pattern has generally been to check references by phone, but I would recommend that you steer clear of this and instead meet with referees in person. If this is not feasible, then use Skype or FaceTime. You establish more of a rapport when you can see someone's face and look them in the eye. Observing facial expressions often adds another dimension to the conversation. At the start, you need to explain to the referee that this is an important conversation – never mind that this might seem dramatic. You should thank them for taking the time to help you get to know the candidate well, as their knowledge is of importance to the candidate's career as well as to his prospective employer. You are communicating to them that unlike other reference checks they may be familiar with, they should not treat this meeting as a cursory unreflective conversation; they should be prepared to answer detailed questions.

To Confirm or to Scrutinise, That Is the Pitfall

As a rule, checking references is done in the final stages of the selection process. By then, the candidate will have undergone several rounds of interviews. The decision-makers will be familiar with his past achievements, what makes him tick, his potential. He's made a good impression on them and the chemistry with the staff is good. The reference check? Important, of course – who would deny that? But in fact it will be perfunctory, more than anything else to confirm what the senior executives have become convinced of during the selection process. This is perfectly understandable and altogether human. Having gone through the interview grind probably with several people, you do not want to find out that you have made the wrong judgment. That it's back to the drawing board. Still, you should resist the temptation to rush through this final stage, and take time to scrutinise your decision. It can be helpful to ask appropriate questions. More on appropriate questions a little later in this chapter.

Listening On and Off

Another pitfall at this stage of the process is the inclination to make light of any critical comments about the candidate, even when they are reasonable. I call this listening on and off – simply hearing what you want to hear and ignoring anything else. I admit that I stumbled into this trap myself in the early years of my career. A professional acquaintance introduced me to a candidate, and I ended up asking for references. If I had read between the lines, I would have seen that the candidate's expert qualifications notwithstanding, people at his current company found him all but impossible to work with. Everyone at his current position felt perpetually upended – he would never stop demanding their attention and would project his stress onto everyone around him. But we were thrilled to have found a suitable candidate for this position, the required qualifications being exceptionally rare. Plus there were virtually no other candidates to be found, which is why I was unmoved by the warning signals. That's why I was tuned in to hearing the positive characteristics of the candidate, of which there were plenty, and ignoring negative reports – a classic beginner's mistake. We were lucky that the second referee we spoke to was far more outspoken about the negative behaviour of the candidate. There was no possible way for us to ignore the bad news.

WHO SPEAKS TO THE REFEREES?

In my mind, the people who conducted interviews are the ones who should check references. If they are doing the job in a professional manner interviewers will want to measure their interview observations against the feedback given by the people who have experience of the candidate *in situ*. The reference check allows dispassionate interviewers to dig deeper. While there is always the risk of confirmation bias, delegating this important step to other colleagues will inevitably leave room for interpretation and for nothing more than a cursory check.

I have even come across organisations where they not only delegate reference checks to people who have never met the candidate, but they give this job to people who have scant experience with or knowledge of the field the candidate is being considered for. Occasionally, reference checks are handed over to junior employees, which I believe is a fundamental error. It's unfair and unrealistic to expect them to have the maturity and experience to ask pointed questions. But the ability to drill down for meaningful information when asking someone for a reference is nothing short of vital.

Apart from the previously described qualifications for making a reference check, it makes sense to bear in mind the personality of the person doing this check. For a report to have substance, this person must be unafraid of asking probing questions. This skill has more to do with personality than with expertise: I know several people who are unable to perform tough reference checks, though their work performance is outstanding in other respects. Whatever the reason – a dominant need for affiliation, a dislike of contentious or antagonistic situations, shyness – they should not be thrust into a painful and unproductive role.

While I am a staunch advocate of never outsourcing reference search, I realise there are times when companies have to do just that. In such cases there are specialist consultants who can do a credible reference-vetting job for you.

Though they have never met the candidate, they have such dedicated specialist experience with references that they can arrive at a realistic observation. So if there is some pressing reason why you cannot reference-check yourself, bring in a specialist consultant to do it for you.

WHICH QUESTIONS SHOULD YOU ASK, AT THE VERY LEAST?

Over the past few years, reference questions have become a popular topic for newspaper and magazine articles, as a quick search engine check will bear out. To draw up the sample list below I have combined some questions from experts in the field with several of our own devising which have proved effective. First however, I suggest that you map out which areas your reference check questions should focus on, lest you leave out important topics. Here are question categories you should keep in mind:

- Questions pertaining to candidate/referee context
- Questions pertaining to achievements
- Questions about personality
- Questions about learning agility, introspection and adaptability
- Questions about dedication and drive or motivation
- Questions in which you request advice
- Questions pertaining to integrity

Some Examples

Here are some examples of reference questions in the categories mentioned above, all of which will boost your knowledge of a candidate whom we'll call Claire:

- **Questions pertaining to context:** What was Claire's job description; how long and when did you work together? What was your working relationship? *This question may seem obvious, but it is essential. First off, you need to know if the referee worked with the candidate for long enough, to form a sound opinion. This is often the first mistake made during the reference check, as people are wont to assume things automatically.*
- **Questions pertaining to achievements:** Could you share with me what Claire achieved at work, and what she excelled at? How well did she hold up under pressure? When did she fail to meet her targets, and why? Could you give me some examples of how she executed her work?

- **Questions about personality:** What can you tell me of Claire's personality? How would you describe her as a person, what are her values? What impression did her colleagues, team members and management have of her? What kind of leader is she, does she collaborate with people, how does she communicate with clients and colleagues? *This last question can provide important information about a candidate's personality. You should make sure your observations of the candidate take personality and spirit of co-creation into account. It is fatal not to, after all: candidates are hired for what they can do, yet fired for who they are!*

- **Questions about learning agility, introspection and adaptability:** What would you say are Claire's best qualities? *Compare this answer with the first three criteria demonstrating learning agility. The chapter on step 6 has the information you need to do this.* Did Claire offer many innovative ideas, and which ones left a lasting impression? Did she often step forward to accept extra projects or responsibilities while she was working for you? *This question can give you an idea of the candidate's adaptability.* Regarding introspection, did Claire often ask for feedback proactively? What did she do with feedback, particularly if she was criticised and several flaws were pinpointed? Was she able to acknowledge her successes and failures in equal measure? *Recruiting agile talent implies that you ask questions relating to agility in all its guises.*

- **Questions about dedication and motive:** To which fields of expertise was Claire most dedicated? How could you tell? What kind of projects did she volunteer for outside the constraints of her job description? What is Claire motivated by? *It is essential that you explain what you are looking for: you want to find out what motivates her, not what she knows and is capable of. In other words, what makes her tick.*

- **Questions in which you request advice:** What score would you give Claire for overall job performance, on a scale of 1 to 10? *What I love about this question is that it compels people to be outspoken. Very often, people will give Claire a solid 8. Your rebuttal question can then be: what does Claire need to be given a perfect 10? The answer will then paint a vivid picture of what Claire's areas needing improvement are. This is a clever way to discover specific, different and more in-depth aspects than you would have found, if you had simply asked after her key areas of improvement.* How well do you think Claire will perform, in the position and context I have just described? Do you think she will be successful in our organisation, and why? *Of course, you cannot ask this question* *until you have offered an accurate description of the position for which Claire is being considered. This should include its responsibilities and tasks, the company strategy and the company culture. When you engage someone in a candidate's case study and ask them for advice, very few people will resist. In fact, most people asked will endeavour to provide detailed answers.*

- **Questions pertaining to integrity:** Would you have Claire deal with the most confidential aspects of your business? *Or, as a variation on the same theme:* Is Claire someone you can trust with your life, professionally speaking? Would you have her take over control of the finances, if you ever had to be out of the country on business for months? How would Claire's close colleagues score her on a scale from 1 to 10? Do you agree with their score and why?
- *Finally, in every single reference check, I ask the referee:* Would you recruit the candidate for the same job again, or for a different one, if the opportunity occurred?

CONCLUSION

By taking the steps suggested in this chapter, you will find that reference checks can provide useful information that will round out the data you have garnered from the other selection tools you have used. It bears repeating: a first-rate reference check can preclude the hiring of otherwise talented people who would nevertheless be a misfit in your organisation.

Over the course of his career, Claudio Fernández-Aráoz – a partner at executive search firm Egon Zehnder and a regular contributor to *Harvard Business Review* – can recall only two instances of having to fire people he had recruited. The secret to his success? "Great reference checking. It is the most important step in making sure that you're not about to bring on board someone who you'll soon want to let go."

FURTHER READING

ARTICLES

- Claudio Fernández-Aráoz (February 11, 2016). "The Right Way to Check a Reference." *Harvard Business Review*.
- Jorg Stegemann (April 28, 2014). "How to Do a Reference Check." Kennedyexecutive.com.

PART 3. PITFALLS, LISTS AND TALENT RETENTION

By now, you have gone through the 9 steps with your selection team and you all have a clear understanding of the candidates. Now it's decision time. In a dedicated session for evaluating, or calibrating as it is sometimes called, everyone can share their opinions, backed up by their rationales. Afterwards, all the elements you are going to base your decision on will be assembled: the completed feedback forms, the reference checks, and any results from tests or assessments, they are all gathered up. Weighing your inputs to decide which candidate is the most appropriate is next.

All the candidates are given clear and concise feedback (this includes the information from the reference checks). Based on the selection methods, you will be capable of clarifying the reason for hiring a particular candidate, or rejecting others. Most candidates are relieved that the selection process was professional, even when told they are not the one for the job. Constructive criticism does not go to waste. Google is a prime example of this: a full 80 percent of rejected candidates would encourage their friends to apply for a position at the organisation.

The calibration session is an opportune time to evaluate the selection process itself and to tweak it if necessary, as all the interested parties have gathered together. This session is an effective way to determine who is good at recruitment and which selection tools have proven useful. Long term, I always recommend that my clients regularly review the achievements of new recruits and compare their performance with the original selection criteria and the decision to hire. This cumulative information will also improve the selection process.

The best and the brightest can only be found after walking a long and winding road, full of obstacles, traps and pitfalls. What might initially seem crucial, can turn out to be of minor significance. Based on my research and practical experience, I am convinced that this concise how-to-guide and its nine steps will help you to select even more, and even better, agile and future-proof talent. The following part of the book will deal with tempting hurdles, offer a handful of tips from business leaders and a sneak peek into the future of search and recruitment.

TEMPTING HURDLES

"The problem with the world is that the intelligent people are full of doubt, while the stupid ones are full of confidence."

CHARLES BUKOWSKI, AMERICAN AUTHOR AND POET

As noted earlier, structured interviews paired with a feedback form can underline the objectivity of interviewers' observations. After all, you are only permitted to score those qualities or prerequisites which you decided were core selection factors, were non-negotiable or were an obstacle to hiring. Any other observations should have no bearing on your decision.

The reason for being so thoroughly committed to objectivity is that people have an innate tendency to see things which do not exist, or to make baseless assumptions. Yes, your observations can be influenced, you are only human. But having some idea of the theoretical reasons behind this all-too-human tendency might help to lessen its impact on your objectivity. In this chapter, I will share several of the hurdles we often come across at our firm.

THE PRINCIPLE OF THE FIRST LIEUTENANT

It is common for talented people to be employed by outstanding companies alongside excellent colleagues. The odds of collaborating with peers who might impart a wealth of knowledge are vastly increased at this kind of organisation. However, this phenomenon has its downside, unexpected and obscure though it may be. People who work for excessively brilliant businesses or for managers with a sterling reputation might sometimes be impacted in a negative sense. Let us assume that the organisation has a distinctive and innovative strategy, or that its reputation for business development is unparalleled in the industry. The leading executive is usually the one who gets all the credit. This is rarely with foundation, for a large part of that executive's achievement was in fact facilitated by the people in his team.

Steve Jobs, founder of Apple, is a prime example of this. A visionary thinker. His design sense was unsurpassed, as was his rare ability for having consumers purchase products they had never imagined needing before. Creating new products, services and even markets, his impact on endless traditional business models knew no equal. He was superlatively gifted. He was often credited with characteristics which he absolutely lacked. It is even worse, though. His inadequacies and areas of indifference were counterbalanced by several managers who reported directly to him. Yet they never received any outward appreciation.

A key example is the supposed brilliant interview skills of Jobs. I remember hearing a radio interview where someone described Jobs as having an unparalleled eye for talent and exceptional interviewing finesse. This could not have been further from the truth. Jobs was known to be very impatient, to the point of being brusque. Anyone who had not managed to leave a dazzling impression in the first three minutes of the interview, was then disregarded by the Apple exec; he did not even pretend to hide his disgust. Luckily, there were numerous people in his team and in the HR department who could make up for this behaviour.

HALOES AND HORNS

Anytime you meet someone for the first time, you build a mental impression of them. Studies have proven that our first impression tends to impact the image we have of someone. The so-called Halo effect occurs when the appearance of a single positive characteristic leads the interviewer to assume there are other good qualities as well. The Horn effect is when the opposite occurs: negative traits are presumed to exist, based on the observation of a single negative aspect. An example might be someone sitting for an entrance exam at a prestigious business school. One of the professors notices the candidate is doing very well on the first test, with not a single mistake to be found. If that same professor later examined the test the candidate completed on a different topic, and he spotted an incorrect answer, he might assume that this was an inadvertent mistake on the part of the student. The professor might leave that incorrect answer out of his final judgment.

CLONE-PICKING

The human tendency to hire people who are like us is one of the hardest pitfalls to avoid. *Similarity attraction* is the term psychologists use. It comes down to us having a strong preference for talent that resembles us. Inversely, talented individuals with different or complementary skills and personality traits are often rejected, or do not even make the first cut of the selection process. Honestly, this is downright foolish in a world that needs more diversity and flexibility. Cloning personalities and skills simply adds up to more of the same. It will prevent you from considering things from different angles.

As rational as this may seem, it often happens inadvertently. Hardly anyone is immune to this. If you are interested in testing your own involuntary prejudices – for gender, ethnicity and age – I would suggest you take the online Harvard Implicit Association Test (IAT).* Odds are you will be more prejudiced than you think, just as I was.

DERAILERS AHEAD!

Numerous lists and countless management books abound on the qualities which characterise talented managers and leaders. My own book *Toptalent* examines nine common criteria typical of the hugely talented. I gleaned these from my personal experience on the job and from sixty interviews with CEOs and supervisory board members. These criteria may be typical for talent, to the point of being universal (what varies is merely the extent to which someone has them), and they may have some predictive validity. However, people tend to forget that too much of these criteria can be overkill, simply too much of a good thing, and fatal for an organisation.

These derailers are difficult to avoid altogether, for ultimately they are the downside of key factors of growth and prosperity. Charisma and self-confidence, for instance, can easily turn to arrogance or a lack of introspection if they are overdeveloped. Another example is people who cannot listen and who are inclined to simply "broadcast" information all the time instead of interacting. This characteristic is the polar opposite of empathy and compassion. All of us can surely think of someone who fits that image. The person who comes to mind for me, is a very clever manager who remains convinced that he is more intelligent than everyone else, because of his exceptional IQ. As a result,

* The IAT is available on the Harvard website. https://implicit.harvard.edu/implicit/takeatest.html

he thinks everyone around him is automatically more stupid. This kind of behaviour is a typical display of inadequate self-awareness; it is the mirror image of one of the key characteristics of talent everywhere: learning agility!

Even the most positive traits can easily become dysfunctional if there is an excess. Everyone who manages other people needs empathy. If you had no empathy, you would have no clue as to what makes people tick, nor would you be able to affect them, never mind inspire and motivate them. Those are essential qualities for any manager. Too much empathy, on the other hand, can cause someone to postpone and avoid tough decisions. This is a well-researched fact. Tough decisions are part of management; all managers will have to make them over the course of their career. My book *How to Become CEO?* illustrates that CEOs and top executives are often inclined to failure due to a lack of knowledge regarding their own pitfalls and derailers. For this reason, every interview needs to determine a candidate's assets as well as how strong these qualities are. All CEOs should have a dominant need for influence, to a certain extent, though if this need for power is too strong, it can lead them to destructive and narcissistic behaviour. The TAT-test mentioned earlier defines four different stages of power and can signal narcissistic behaviour.

CONCLUSION
Talent selection is complicated and subjective. Despite our collective assumption that we are discerning and self-reliant, life throws many distractions our way. This chapter has discussed some less familiar pitfalls and temptations. There are scores of other outside influences that will impact our observation. The best way to prevent massive errors is to gain some theoretical understanding and to use the focused interview paired with a feedback form.

FURTHER READING

BOOKS

- Larry J. Bloom (2012). *The Cure for Corporate Stupidity. Avoid the Mind-Bugs that Cause Smart People to Make Bad Decisions.* Xmente.
- David L. Dotlich & Peter C. Cairo (2003). *Why CEOs Fail. The 11 Behaviors That Can Derail Your Climb to the Top and How to Manage Them.* Jossey-Bass.
- Phil Rosenzweig (2014). *The Halo Effect… and the Eight Other Business Delusions That Deceive Managers.* Free Press. Reissue edition.

ARTICLES

- Rod Johnson (March 1, 2016). "The Top 10 Leadership Derailers and How to Best Mitigate Those Risks." Growingyourleaders.com.
- Joyce E.A. Russell (February 7, 2014). "Career Coach: Are Your Derailers Holding You Back?" *The Washington Post.*

WARREN BUFFETT, JEFF BEZOS AND DEE HOCK: THEIR LISTS

"What we spend our time on is probably the most important decision we make."

RAY KURZWEIL, JOINT FOUNDER OF SINGULARITY UNIVERSITY

Successful business owners and managers alike understand that selecting the right talent is essential to their success. They know that just having the right skill set is virtually never sufficient. A unique blend of ability, needs and identity is what really matters. This chapter will share personal recommendations from the most prosperous investor on the planet, the CEO of online retail giant Amazon and the highly innovative founder and former CEO of Visa.

WARREN BUFFETT, INVESTOR EXTRAORDINAIRE, AND HIS THREE CRITERIA

Investor Warren Buffett is famously fond of simplifying issues. His checklist for selecting the very best talent is a prime example of simplification. When he is looking to recruit new associates the American billionaire believes that there are essentially just three things that count: "You look for three qualities: integrity, intelligence, and energy. And if you don't have the first, the other two will kill you. If you hire somebody without integrity, you really want them to be dumb and lazy."

JEFF BEZOS AND HIS THREE ROUTINE QUESTIONS

The American company Amazon is one of the businesses revolutionising online retail. There may be more than one reason for its success, but CEO Jeff Bezos is positive that selecting the very best staffers is hugely important. "It would be impossible to produce results in an environment as dynamic as the Internet without extraordinary people. Setting the bar high in our approach to hiring has been, and will continue to be, the single most important element of Amazon's success."

Bezos asks three questions in every interview and he has charged his managers to do the same. He believes these questions have made all the difference:

1. **Will you admire this person?** Bezos's first benchmark was about admiration. He wanted hiring managers to admire anyone they were bringing onto their teams. He meant that this was a person who could be an example to others and from whom others could learn. Based on this criterion alone, the standard for hiring is kept sky high.

2. **Will this person raise the average level of effectiveness of the group they are entering?** Jeff Bezos declares there is one clear reason for new hires: elevating the company. That is what it is all about. The bar has to continuously go up, to prevent apathy growing as the company grows. To test people, Bezos asks them to visualise the company five years from now. At that point, each of us should look around and say, "The standards are so high now – boy, I'm glad I got in when I did!"

3. **Along which dimensions might this person be a superstar?** The last and possibly quirkiest thing Bezos seeks from new hires is a distinctive skill or interest to contribute to the company's culture and help cultivate a fun and interesting workplace. And it doesn't have to be related to the job. While there's a lot to be said for being well-rounded, it's the pointy types Bezos wants.[*]

Even though Bezos' list is now 15 years old, Amazon has come a long way thanks to this hiring strategy. His three questions may not cover everything you ever want to know, but they will upgrade your selection process as quirky and original additions to the traditional questions you should ask anyway, in every interview.

---

[*] Excerpts from Vernon Gunnarson, "3 Questions Amazon CEO Jeff Bezos Asks Before Hiring Anyone." Inc.com.

DEE HOCK, AND HIS LIST FOR TOMORROW'S LEADERS

Former Visa CEO Dee Hock was another CEO who invested time in drawing up an extensive checklist to search and recruit superlative talent. I believe that everyone with an interest in all aspects of the search for excellence ought to immerse themselves in Hock's thinking. His checklist may have been conceived 20 years ago, but it is as up-to-date now as it was then. He was particularly ahead of his time with his focus on learning agility.

Like Buffett, Dee Hock knew that integrity is the bedrock of a successful hire. His list of priorities for the hiring and promoting of staff that is a little bit more elaborate than Buffett's. Hock believes the recipe for finding the very best people consists of these 6 steps: "Hire and promote first on the basis of integrity; second, motivation; third, capacity; fourth, understanding; fifth, knowledge; and last and least, experience. Without integrity, motivation is dangerous; without motivation, capacity is impotent; without capacity, understanding is limited; without understanding, knowledge is meaningless; without knowledge, experience is blind."

CONCLUSION

Successful business owners and managers alike understand that selecting superlatively talented people is essential. They have made their own lists of key success factors. I would suggest you do the same. Keep track of what worked well, in the selection sessions you were involved in. Are there any particular characteristics that keep popping up and merit special attention on your list? Draw up a first draft and check these characteristics against observations from other selection team members. Be sure to return to the list frequently to tweak it. Be bold in ranking the characteristics. Such lists can show you – in generic terms – how to set priorities in selection. Remember though, they are not to take the place of the specific criteria for a position. What they do instead, is help you understand which generic factors have the greatest predictive validity regarding future success.

FURTHER READING

BOOKS

- Richard J. Connors (2010). *Warren Buffett on Business. Principles from the Sage of Omaha.* John Wiley & Sons.
- Dee Hock & Peter M. Senge (2005). *One from Many. VISA and the Rise of Chaordic Organization.* Berrett-Koehler Publishers.
- Brad Stone (2013). *The Everything Store. Jeff Bezos and the Age of Amazon.* Little, Brown and Company.

ARTICLES

- Vernon Gunnarson. "3 Questions Amazon CEO Jeff Bezos Asks Before Hiring Anyone." Inc.com.
- M. Mitchell Waldrop (1996). "Dee Hock on Management." Fastcompany.com.

RETAINING AGILE TALENT

"Train your people well enough so they can leave, treat them well enough so they don't want to."

RICHARD BRANSON

I hope that the step-by-step guide and recommendations of this book will help you recruit a new generation of agile and future-proof talent. The good news: even a handful of superlative agile talented people will have a profound effect on your business and its results. Besides, if they match most of the criteria we have discussed in this book, they will provide you with sustained achievements and they are potentially – in theory at least – going to be with you for the long haul. The bad news: this is just the beginning. All too frequently, I have noticed companies go to extreme lengths to recruit the *best, the brightest and the most adaptive to change* talented individuals, only to end up surprised and disappointed when they proceeded to leave again in the blink of an eye.

What are some of the ingredients that might entice or incite people to commit to a company? A detailed answer to this question packs enough substance to fill another book, yet I believe it to be too significant not to give a hint of it now.

HOW TO RETAIN THEM?
If you are serious about retaining agile (top) talent, there are several things you can do. The list includes – though is certainly not limited to – the following elements:
1. **Develop an onboarding mindset.** First, let them get their bearings.
2. **Remember: captivating beats captivity.** A lot of startups have found this to be true; talented people might simply be motivated by money. To deal with this, the startup will offer them money to leave the company directly after being hired.

3. **Put people before protocol.** In other words, beware of letting your company ossify into a pattern of rigid protocols for everything. One size does not fit all.
4. **Make check-ins frequent and one-to-one.** It's important to keep in touch – but not to micromanage.
5. **Compare company purpose to individual needs and values.** Company purpose should be more than advertising slogans – ideally speaking you should compare if it aligns with the values of individual staff members.
6. **Give them challenging projects within and outside the company.**
7. **Ask for their strategic input ("what") and give them executive freedom ("how").** Be sure to give them proper targets to achieve, though. Freedom does not equal "no strings attached".

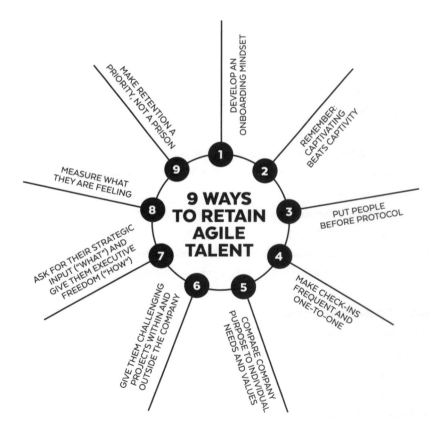

8. Measure what they are feeling. Preferably all the time, or as often as is practicable, and at least in real time (without delay, that is). There are various tools to help you do this.

9. Make retention a priority, not a prison.

1. Develop an Onboarding Mindset

Organisations often spend an immense amount of time on selecting people, yet once they start work there is insufficient attention paid to showing them the ropes with a proper entry programme. Sometimes this is due to budget constraints, but all too often onboarding is a victim of ignorance – "We're sure that new hire of ours will be able to cope," management says. New employees end up having to find their own way, often a time-consuming process, and mutually frustrating. Step one for talent **retention**, then, is to help them as they find their bearings in your organisation.

For solid advice on setting up your onboarding programme I recommend George Bradt's book *Onboarding. How to Get Your New Employees Up to Speed in Half the Time*. Bradt, an associate of mine, is an executive onboarding expert, writer for Forbes.com, and author of four books on the subject. *Onboarding. How to Get Your New Employees Up to Speed in Half the Time* is essential reading, bursting with ideas for setting up a practical and hands-on onboarding programme. The first important step is to make an individually-tailored onboarding plan. Employers need to ensure that the candidate will have the right tools at their fingertips, can access any relevant informal networks and begin to understand the company culture. Onboarding should not be considered as a brief "intro to the company" phase. The need – and benefits – last for (much) longer than you might expect.

"Financial incentives should not be excessive […] And external incentives like money work only in conjunction with internal motivators like the need for achievement and recognition."

FERNÁNDEZ-ARÁOZ, GROYSBERG & NOHRIA,
HARVARD BUSINESS REVIEW, WINTER 2012

---

2. Remember: Captivating Beats Captivity

The next step: you want to *captivate* people – get them to commit to and to stay interested in your organisation. Holding them *captive* – making them feel they have to stay because their salary and the bonus plan are so lucrative – is something else entirely.

Over the course of my career, I have come across many different ways of awarding bonuses. I am not opposed to the financial incentive of a bonus, if it falls within reason. However, I believe that it is simplistic to equate people's level of commitment with the size of their paycheques alone. A person with a strong need for affiliation (see step 2 of this book) will not find much incentive in a bonus. This type of person is eager to build relationships and achieve results as a team. They feel distinctly uncomfortable with incentives that differentiate between individuals.

It is for this very reason that I have more faith in making people interested than in getting them to commit. Dutch author Quintin Schevernels, who wrote *Suits & Hoodies* (only available in Dutch), spent much time investigating start-ups and scale-ups and he found a wider truth: although many employees at these companies like to be challenged in their jobs, and some of them might be fulfilled by working for a higher (social) purpose, even at hipster tech businesses, you can come across "fortune-hunters".

In response to this drawback, several successful tech companies have made the smart move of offering strong candidates two options at the end of the selection process: either sign a contract of employment, or refuse the job and be rewarded with a lump sum. In a related practice American online retailer Zappos pays one thousand dollars to staffers who decide to quit after working for them for one week. This is a smart way to find out if someone is motivated by money above all else, or if he is truly driven to dedicate himself to the joint challenge of the company goals and collegial relationships. Fun fact: this unorthodox policy generates some interesting PR for Zappos, as well.

If you would prefer to keep your agile talent engaged, you need to appeal to their thirst for knowledge. You should create a corporate atmosphere conducive to autonomy, creativity, flexibility and innovation. An atmosphere and culture where it is acceptable to make mistakes and where new ideas are hailed with a warm welcome. We'll discuss one specific way to increase the odds of people staying interested in number 5 below.

3. Put People before Protocol

Even organisations with a proactive policy for retention can lose their focus. A classic mistake in talent retention is to assume that one size fits all, that you need not tailor the programme to individuals. But people are individuals first, with wildly divergent personal needs and their own unique personalities. We would love there to be a generic maxim to keep people with us, but we intrinsically know that people's preferences are often very different. Management-development programmes that try and force one style of leadership are a good example. The same reasoning applies to retention programmes based on a universal methodology, which will prove ineffective. Standardised Management Development programmes simply produce inauthentic, karaoke-style leadership. Agile talents are especially turned off by this uninspired and boring nonsense. Standardised retention programmes will be equally useless in getting your best people to commit to your organisation.

By definition, agile talent is flexible and mercurial, and generally feels uncomfortable and stifled by standardised procedures and programmes. The answer: a retention programme tailored to the individual, which you check regularly and keep adjusting, if needed.

"Agility and the myth of controllability are on opposite sides of the table. Retention once meant a strictly planned method geared at keeping your very best talent close. It would however be foolish to stick to this too rigidly. I recommend regular checks and adjusting your course of action accordingly. After all, agility and the retention of agile talent are all about being nimble and thinking on your feet."

WILLEMIJN BOSKMA, AGILE SCRUM COACH AND ADVISER AT SCRUM COMPANY

4. Make Check-ins Frequent and One-to-One

It makes sense to check in frequently – to discover how that talented individual finds inspiration– than to simply assume what will work. Just ask them! It is preferable to do this in person, stopping by for regular chats to check in. The conversation should have an open vibe to it, and not resemble a traditional interview or standardised Q&A session. It needs to be a contemporary dialogue, a chance for people to open up and give and receive feedback on their vision of collaboration, of shared purpose and of mutual expectations. It is important to discuss areas where staffer and employer can both thrive, but conversations about areas needing improvement should not be avoided.

5. Compare Company Purpose to Individual Needs and Values

We have previously discussed the myth of controllability. The same applies to malleability. We are fond of thinking that primary needs and intrinsic values are malleable, yet this idea is unfounded, as research has shown time and again. Upon reaching adolescence, our values and needs have largely solidified. It makes more sense, then, to see what are the dominant values and needs of an individual and compare these to the company's core values. If they are nearly completely aligned, then the odds increase that someone will feel inspired doing their work. Gradually, more businesses are applying agile working principles and they prioritise matching company culture and its values with those of prospective hires when they search and recruit people.

6. Give Them Challenging Projects Within and Outside the Company

I can understand how tempting it is to select a person who knows all the aspects of a position inside out; but I know this to be a disastrous course of action for recruiting talent. This is particularly true in trying to recruit truly outstanding individuals. Companies often want to find qualified talent, but then try to entice the person to do something they have done many times before. In fact, the new position is basically the sum of the parts of their prior experience, rejigged to fit a slightly smaller organisation or one of equal size and complexity as their current job. But agile talent feels motivated by the exact opposite of the "comfortable slippers" syndrome. Eager to learn, they love to push boundaries and are excessively fond of working on projects teeming with new and unexpected challenges. As a company, you are better off presenting them with a position familiar in some respects, yet offering plenty of challenges to leap over their comfort zone.

Push and Provoke Them

"You need to find a context where you are on firm footing – metaphorically speaking – on one leg, and lost in darkness on the other one. In other words, to push yourself out of your comfort zone there needs to be the right balance of knowns and new things to learn." This is what Hans Wijers, former CEO of Akzo Nobel N.V., a Dutch multinational company, and currently supervisory board member for numerous organisations, once told me about talent.

If you have talented people work on projects that they can just barely cope with, they not only experience a far steeper learning curve, they will enjoy themselves much more in the process. When I think of retaining talent, I can't help recalling the freewheeling and non-regimented heroine of the Pippi Longstocking stories. Pippi, brimming with self-confidence, has an attitude that seems to say: "I have never tried that before, so I think I should definitely be able to do it!"

Access to the Very Best People

Another way of stretching agile talent beyond their limits is to have them work with the very best. This type of talent has been selected for their curiosity and learning agility, among other attributes. They absolutely relish the opportunity to work with people from whom they have much to learn. It is crucial to let them work with such people, every day, in their own team. Alternatively, you could place them in a member-shifting workgroup – irrespective of position –

where they can again interact with the very best. This can be done within the organisation, or outside. Henk Smit, a partner in Advisory Practice in the Netherlands branch of KPMG, invests some of his time in the Dutch NGO Alzheimer LAB. This is a programme conceived when several CEOs brainstormed to figure out how they could make a meaningful contribution to the Dutch Alzheimer Foundation. Smit devised the plan that the participating organisations would each have two of their top talents take part in the project for two full years. As a result the project is given input from the very best people, and talented individuals are given the opportunity to collaborate with other brilliant individuals, all for the benefit of dealing with an important issue in society. They return inspired and invigorated by the experience. If you wish to keep your agile talent interested, why don't you start thinking outside of the corporate box like this? I'm sure there are good opportunities near you for setting up interesting projects outside the company!

7. Ask for Their Strategic Input ("What") and Give Them Executive Freedom ("How")

There are few (agile) talents around who do not love the challenge of difficult or new issues. They cannot wait to tap into their creative spirit and use their learning agility, and they enjoy nothing better than contributing to the development of new business models and innovative strategies. They are absolutely repulsed by routine and repetition, and hate working in surroundings which dictate how they should execute their job down to the last detail. Once you have offered them the opportunity to input strategy, it makes sense to find a consensus on what the results should be. The next step: give them full discretion, in keeping with the corporate values of course, as to how they achieve these results. Involve them in the "what", and allow them a lot of freedom, as to "how" they achieve it. Challenge them on substance, but set them free to do their job following their star.

8. Measure What They Are Feeling

One of the most common failures in their attempt to retain agile talent occurs when managers project the generic onto individual standards for challenges and growth. I remember making that mistake early in my career. One of the offices of the firm I then worked for was being run by a young, freshly graduated, highly talented technical business expert. Disregarding his enormous thirst for knowledge, his swift rise through the company and his talent for successfully juggling numerous tasks and responsibilities, I simply assumed that he would stick around in that role for a short but significant period of time. My assumption was based on precedent: previous managers tended to fill that position for a couple of years before moving on to the next. My judgment call proved to be erroneous; he left us to work for an American strategist firm where his learning curve would be stimulated and nourished and he would be able to further his career. I should not have assumed he was satisfied just purring along. I rather should have checked in with him regularly, to find out if he was still sufficiently stimulated by his projects.

Here is more evidence of the importance of keeping track of employee engagement:

- A 2013 study by Towers Watson* found that, in organisations with strong employee satisfaction scores, the financial results are a stunning 300 percent higher than those at less happy businesses. A Gallup poll**, also from 2013, shows that a mere 13 percent of employees worldwide are completely satisfied with and feel fully committed to their job. As an employer, reading the tealeaves of this sort is nothing short of urgent.
- A study conducted by the Intelligence Group*** shows 64 percent of millennials saying they would prefer to earn $40,000 annually doing work that makes them happy, to earning $100,000 a year in a job that makes them miserable.
- Belgian entrepreneur Raymond Hannes and his team at Vita.io have developed an app which lets staffers and organisations alike measure, understand and work on what makes them happy on the job. The app sends out several messages a day to employees, and the recipient is free to decide whether to interact. The staffer can then have a conversation through the app, with a personalised chatbot. The aim of this discussion is to determine that employee's main happiness factor at work. Often, someone has trouble being specific about this in normal conversations. The idea behind Vita.io is that people experience happiness at work if it empowers them and takes place in an atmosphere of growth, where they feel fulfilled by their work. These aspects fit in an easy acronym: AMO, which stands for Ability, Motivation and

---

*   *Global Workforce Study 2012*, by Towers Watson.
**   Steve Crabtree (October 8, 2013). "Worldwide, 13% of Employees are Engaged at Work." Gallup.com.
*** Morley Winograd & Michael Hais (May 2014). *How Millennials Could Upend Wall Street and Corporate America*. Governance Study at Brookings.

Opportunity. Employee and employer can both use the app. Vita.io has made it possible to produce real-time information on employee and company satisfaction. This in turn will help businesses to be more responsive. Vita.io can develop tailor-made interventions for companies.

9. Make Retention a Priority, Not a Prison

Sometimes, even if you have followed the eight instructions in this chapter thoroughly, the best agile talent is going to leave you. Their rare and future-proof blend of traits makes them interesting to other employers, who might manage to woo them regardless of all the personal attention and appreciation you have heaped upon them. The unique blend of curiosity, learning agility and eagerness for feedback makes these talented individuals extremely inclined to keep their eyes peeled for new and greener pastures.

When you lose a valued employee your only course of action is to double down on your commitment to engage the other agile talent in your organisation. Make sure their job is as interesting, diverse and exciting as can be. Have them work on ground-breaking projects, or introduce them to brilliant people, from whom they can learn a huge amount, whatever their position in the company.

"The one thing agile talent appreciates above all else is having immediate and informal access to the most challenging projects, working in an atmosphere free of hierarchy, and collaborating with brilliant colleagues."

If, however, in one of your frequent conversations they tell you that they are planning to leave, be sure not to pout and be petulant. Listen carefully instead. And look at how other companies, Google for example, take this problem in stride.

Google aims to help people like this as best they can, by coaching them and helping them to assess how realistic their plans are. For instance: a staffer who indicates he is planning to set up his own business will be asked why he wants to leave the organisation and whether his plans are at all sound and practical. If these are not yet up to scratch, so to speak, the company will give him all the help and room that he needs, to perfect the business plan. Of course, Google will do anything to keep him on board. Still, if it is a brilliant plan, they are not going to stand in his way and instead opt to invest in a lasting, positive relationship with the departing staffer. This could include a great send-off, or the offer to invest in the startup, and warmly welcome them to the club for Google alumni, at the very least. I witnessed this kind of happy goodbye several times myself, where the parting of ways does in fact produce a wonderful outside ambassador of the company. Your organisation is highly recommended to others, or they may even bring business opportunities to you, from their new position. This principle of onboarding, keeping people on board and positive exit-strategies does not merely apply to lower and middle management, but is relevant for top talent and top executives as well.

FRACTIONAL RETENTION? HERE COME THE "SLASHIES"!

A new term has crept into business jargon recently: "slashie". A slashie is someone who holds down more than one job. There are various reasons that impel people to take on a second occupation. The "pink slip," or being laid off is one unfortunate reason. Losing a well-paying job can cause individuals to take on two or more less prestigious and well-paying jobs, with the consequent slash chopping their professional identity into segments. Aspiring artists and entertainers occupy another segment of the slashie workforce – the young actress working as a waitress until her big break enables her to pay the rent from her theatre income is an example.

WHAT IF WE INVEST
IN DEVELOPING OUR PEOPLE
AND THEY LEAVE US?

WHAT IF WE DON'T
AND THEY STAY?

But there is another group who embrace the slashie lifestyle freely. These are people who feel their many talents and interests are too abundant to fit into one single profession. Nowadays, all sorts of people have several jobs, positions or roles at once – there are even several partners at our firm who fit the description of a slashie, combining various roles at once. In fact, statistics in various countries show that this trend is here to stay.

If someone on your staff or one of your managers has an unfulfilled need to do something else in addition to their day job, you can desperately and frenetically try to keep them to yourself. However, you might also consider letting them become a slashie, cutting back their time with your firm to, say, three days a week. This leaves them with two days in which to explore other options.

CONCLUSION

Retaining talent can be done in several different ways. Studies and real-life experience show that a bespoke approach is more effective than trying to squeeze everyone into a one-size-fits-all mould. You have to give your best talent ample opportunities to explore regions outside of their comfort zone. You need to create challenges for them within or outside the company, to have them (metaphorically speaking) stand on firm footing with one leg while they are floundering in darkness with the other one.

Do your utmost to keep stellar employees with you, but if you can see for yourself that the time has come for them to leave, do not be bitter about it. I have personally experienced how "good leavers" can prove to be outstanding ambassadors for a business, recommending their former employees and even bringing them new business.

The third option, besides staying and leaving, includes the so-called slashie. Traditional companies are still far from becoming accustomed to this phenomenon, though anyone who wishes to retain the brightest and the best ought to make sure they are feeling inspired, invigorated and challenged both on the job and outside work. Chaining talented staffers to the company through long-term bonuses is really just a good way to lull yourself into a false sense of security.

FURTHER READING

BOOKS

- George B. Bradt, Jayme A. Check & John A. Lawler (2016). *The New Leader's 100-Day Action Plan. How to Take Charge, Build or Merge Your Team, and Get Immediate Results.* 4th edition. John Wiley & Sons.
- George B. Bradt & Mary Vonnegut (2009). *Onboarding: How to Get Your New Employees Up to Speed in Half the Time.* John Wiley & Sons.
- Richard P. Finnegan (2015). *The Stay Interview. A Manager's Guide to Keeping the Best and Brightest.* Amacom.
- Beverly Kaye & Sharon Jordan-Evans (2014). *Love 'Em or Lose 'Em. Getting Good People to Stay.* Berrett-Koehler Publishers.
- Jack J. Philips & Adele O. Connell (2011). *Managing Employee Retention. A Strategic Accountability Approach.* Routledge.
- Daniel H. Pink (2010). *Drive. The Surprising Truth About What Motivates Us.* Riverhead Books.

ARTICLES

- Steve Crabtree (October 8, 2013). "Worldwide, 13% of Employees are Engaged at Work." Gallup.com.
- Carol Dweck (January 13, 2016). "What Having a 'Growth Mindset' Actually Means." *Harvard Business Review.*
- Claudio Fernández-Aráoz, Boris Groysberg & Nitin Nohria (October 2011). "How to Hang On to Your High Potentials." *Harvard Business Review.*
- Towers Watson (2012). *Global Workforce Study 2012.*
- Morley Winograd & Michael Hais (May 2014). *How Millennials Could Upend Wall Street and Corporate America.* Governance Studies at Brookings.

EPILOGUE. THE FUTURE OF SEARCH

> **"Software is eating the world, in all sectors. In the future, every company will become a software company."**
>
> MARC ANDREESSEN, FOUNDER OF NETSCAPE

Because the world is in flux and the impact of technology is unprecedented, virtually every industry and business sector will be affected. Essentially, nearly all companies will end up as IT businesses. This phenomenon does not just impact the – relatively traditional – executive search business; it will influence everyone who is involved in the selection of people. Allow me to share a few trends which I believe will become mainstream within the next decade. Potential candidates will be tracked down using data analysis, for instance, and intuition will no longer be the only beacon people use to chart a course in HR and selection procedures. New tools can help you find more facts to test your observations with, as well as provide a more solid foundation for your decisions regarding the candidates. Crunching the numbers will become critical.

BIG DATA AS A TRACKING INSTRUMENT

Several years ago, an international client of ours requested a meeting to discuss the business of international search & recruitment. Our firm was not part of any global conglomerate, which had the client worried, justifiably so, I might add, about the depth of our network in Asia and the United States. This incident forced us to consider our future position.

Subsequently, we decided to fast-track two issues. Besides the obvious move to join an acclaimed international network, we felt it made sense to consider collaborating with companies specialising in big data. As it turned out, there were firms with deep knowledge and expertise in finding the rare gems of top candidates the world over. They had teams of big data-experts, consisting of astronomers, econometrists and mathematicians. They would peruse the digital footprint each of us leaves behind online, to investigate who were the most qualified candidates – in the whole world – for a position. Not limiting themselves to traditional social media like LinkedIn, they would find out who were the keynote speakers at specialist networking events, whose names came up in databases of practice leaders, and so on. In the search key, all the apparently relevant criteria would be gathered up and the search results would then turn up nearly every potential candidate.

As stunning as these results might have been, they did swiftly show a weak spot, too: finding practically anyone was easy, as was checking if candidates were available and willing to relocate. But discovering if candidates in fact had the appropriate social skills, were made of leadership material, etcetera, was not so easy at all. The first stage of the selection process used scientific analysis, the second stage remained – largely – human craftsmanship.

This has now begun to change, with several companies using artificial intelligence as a basis for predictions on candidates' eligibility. Seedlink Tech is a prime example of such a company. To find out more about Seedlink Tech's data-driven approach to talent prediction, I interviewed Rina Joosten-Rabou, cofounder and CCO of this Shanghai-based firm. She explained that Seedlink Tech develops artificial intelligence that can predict – based on language analysis – whether a person might be a good fit for a position and an organisation. Seedlink Tech's software technology employs language analytic algorithms and machine learning to analyse linguistic patterns. The computer brain pairs language, particularly expressions and words, with what can be expected in terms of behaviour and personality. The candidate's "Key Behaviour Benchmarking Profile" is then compared with members of the staff that are recognised as being high performers. Truly exceptional leaders have shared linguistic characteristics, it turns out. Also, each profession builds up its own "culture"; accountants have a different way of speaking than creatives, while bankers who behave "compliantly" tend to say different things and use other phrases than bankers with a riskier profile do.

The same applies to company culture. Broadly speaking, a company's culture is made up of the people who work there. Through their analysis of employees' language, Seedlink Tech can build predictive models for a successful hiring strategy.

RESUME SELECTION HAS SCANT PREDICTIVE VALIDITY!

Anyone involved in selecting talent has been there: ten minutes into an interview, and you just know the magic is not happening. As a courtesy, you finish the ordeal. Afterwards, you sit there stunned, thinking back to how promising the resume had seemed. You should take heart: this happens to us all.

For most organisations, the resume is the first step in the selection process. But let's face it: this first step does not get us very far. Rina Joosten-Rabou explains the advantages of the AI approach: "First of all, there is no predictive validity in a resume, nor does it have any bearing on how someone will perform in their next job. Next, we tend to simplify the selection to a few basic characteristics, such as experience in that industry, or education. These do not cover skills and motivation, though. It is usually not an option to interview every single candidate, due to limited resources. The state of the job market means that it takes, on average, a full year for professionals to find a new job. In some industries, finding talent or retaining it is a real issue. These new technologies, including artificial intelligence, are bringing about positive change to the situation."

In China, recruiters were literally up until midnight, at a French cosmetics company, reviewing thousands of resumes which had been submitted for a handful of positions that needed filling. "We are instinctively aware of the fact that we are bound to miss good people, if we just screen resumes," their recruitment director explained. "We look at the level of education, the university they attended and whether a candidate did an internship at any of our competitors. Despite the fact that it may have been the worst internship in history, candidates are going to be selected on that basis. I am sorry to say that this is all we are able to do, because the number of applicants is too great to schedule personal interviews."

But everything changed when the company began using artificial intelligence to predict which candidates would be the best match for a position and for the company culture, instead of just scanning a resume for key words. Now face-to-face interviews are replaced by digital ones. Candidates are interviewed and then selected by a robot. Yes, I can hear your mind reeling, as you think: "What?! A robot, a machine, selecting the very best talent?" That's right. And we are not talking of 2050, it was in 2014 that the company first started this process. Now, the organisation interviews all 40,000 applicants on their mobile phones, using the questions a recruiter would formerly have asked in a proper interview, to assess their skills. "How do you get people to collaborate?" "What do you mean by good leadership?" "Why do you want to work with us?" Applicants are afforded the opportunity to answer these questions in their own words, using their own ideas, experiences and illustrations.

Source: Seedlink Tech

The research done by Seedlink has shown that our language patterns – the way we speak and what we say – correlate and interact intensely with our behaviour and how we do things. The beauty of language is that it is unconsciously assembled in our brains, our utterances bearing a unique imprint of who we are. And just as we can only see the 10 percent of an iceberg above the water line, its bulk under water invisible to us, our language patterns subsume all the primary needs and personality traits I have mentioned throughout this book. You never know how exceptional a candidate's potential might be merely by scanning a resume and conducting an interview. Much remains below the person's "water line", invisible to the human eye, though these character traits have immense impact on human behaviour and the predictability of future success. But artificial intelligence can reveal the 90 percent which would otherwise remain invisible to our ordinary observations, or to our ears if we could tune in. Cutting-edge businesses have already started adopting this technology to grow their efficiency in making decisions based on data.

Joosten-Rabou clarifies: "One third of candidates selected by the computer proved to have a different background, a different university degree or different work experience to previously selected candidates in prior years. They would not have been selected based on their resumes. Ninety percent of the ultimately-hired candidates initially come recommended by the algorithms from the first step of the selection process. According to line executives, the new hires showed above average achievements. There are 25 percent fewer candidates who quit during their trial period, a clear indication that candidates are far more motivated."

BID YOUR GUT INSTINCT FAREWELL!

Artificial intelligence, big data, and science are going to play a larger and larger role in the search for and recruitment of (top) talent. Interviewers will still be in the driver's seat for a while, making the decisions, but they will soon take it for granted that their decisions are being based on and corroborated by people analytics and smart algorithms.

There are various ways to substantiate your intuition. The method used by Seedlink Tech is just one of these. Another is serious gaming.

Serious Gaming

Hiring is time-consuming. To save time during the hiring process, more companies will turn to video games to evaluate job candidate nuances such as creativity, problem solving, and collaboration. Candidates' game scores will be measured against scores of successful employees, making hard data – alongside subjective opinions from hiring managers – an asset to predict success.

To get an idea of the potential of serious gaming in talent recruitment, let's turn to a Silicon Valley startup called Knack. This San Francisco-based company has released a game called Balloon Brigade. This game allows you to make an initial analysis of the skills and personality traits of a candidate, as well as of areas needing improvement. For example, someone could claim to handle stress well, and to never be plagued by self-doubt. For good measure, the candidate could also claim to be able to inspire others and have an analytical mind. Balloon Brigade can help you to substantiate or refute these claims. The game is deceptively fun, as it contains a wealth of cutting edge science, devised by a multidisciplinary team of scientists from leading universities like Harvard and Yale. They include Alvin Roth, worldwide game theory expert and Nobel Prize winner for Economics in 2012. People analytics, which is a blend of data analysis, theory of probability, psychology and digital technology, helps to validate the decisions regarding candidates.

As deceptively simple as the games by Knack are – rather like this book, come to think of it – they are not just interested in the scores that people get in the game. They also pay attention to how the score was achieved. Hard skills are measured, certainly, but so are social intelligence, creativity and integrity. Besides, the system can also give an idea of the candidate's learning agility.

Smart Badges
As well as serious gaming, there are other newly developed clever tools that can aid you in candidate analysis. Humanyze is a spin-off company of the illustrious Massachusetts Institute of Technology (MIT). They help business to make datasets built around smart badges and algorithms. A smart badge is a variation on the badge that businesses often hand out to visitors of their company. This particular badge can take visual and audio recordings, though.

The badge records how often someone speaks, what their tone of voice is, which networks they participate in professionally, and how productive they are. Humanyze is then able to make all sorts of predictions of future behaviour, all the while staying within the constraints of privacy. (People who would rather not take part in the experiment are given a "placebo-badge", so as not to expose them to peer pressure.) Many countries do not permit this badge at all because of privacy laws. The analyses are sound and valuable however, and the fact remains that tools such as these are now a real possibility.

The statistics here are mostly aggregated, and not individualised. They can help produce more well-founded arguments and decisions in the future. At the very least, you can analyse group behaviour. If you have the appropriate permission from the participants and the legislation of the country permits it, you can also analyse the actions of an individual. The underlying idea is that there is a huge potential for learning in large batches of data.

The IBM initiative known as the Watson project is one example.* Watson will make huge strides in the field of medicine, thanks to a computer collecting all the different experiences of physicians the world over and subsequently calculated. The outcome: a huge wealth of hands-on expertise.

---

* You can find the film *IBM Watson: How It Works* on YouTube:
  https://www.youtube.com/watch?v=_Xcmh1LQB9I

HOW TO SELECT AGILE TALENT FOR THE FORESEEABLE FUTURE

The job market is changing before our very eyes. Jobs change, disappear or are absorbed by new forms of labour, such as the rise of self-employed people or the slashie phenomenon. All these things are moving into the mainstream as we speak. Staffers feel less loyalty to employers, which leads to higher employee turnover, even for executives. When you put this into perspective, it becomes ever more relevant to understand the full profile (ability, motivation, identity) of employees, and thus, their future success.

The way forward is to build a properly structured selection process – using a carefully considered combination of the selection methods in this book, and in relation to each other. It does make sense, though, to utilise all the modern techniques you have at your disposal. When you want to select agile talent, you should apply the future-proof criteria indicated in the illustration on page 181.

We Can All Do Better, But Some of Us Have More Potential

Recruiters are by no means the only ones who can be involved in recruitment. Leaders and managers alike need to be aware of their responsibility – one of their key ones, no less – of selecting the very best staffers. They might add others to the selection team, though I do believe they should always have hands-on involvement when important positions need to be filled. Anyone who takes the time to study the theories on talent selection and has the best people around them to practise with, can hugely improve their selection skills. Practice makes (nearly) perfect, as does feedback from excellent leaders and peers and fine-tuning our plans. Still, some of us have more potential, more of a natural aptitude. The difference between an adequate recruiter and an excellent one is, as always, defined by the unique blend of intelligence, learning agility and – most importantly – the right primary needs and personality traits. For instance, I have come across many smart and experienced interviewers who had a strong need for affiliation. For that very reason, they had trouble confronting candidates with hard questions. Technically, they might be highly proficient interviewers with all the best questions at the ready, and yet, on account of their dominant need, still steer clear of sharply phrased questions. This need not be an issue, though it does drive home the point that you need to be aware of the personality and primary needs of your interviewers in advance. The companies I know who display this awareness are few and far between.

Humans *and* Computers

All these developments will continue to have a greater impact on Human Resources and Recruitment. Specifically, the influence of IT, (big) data and science are likely to grow. Soon, we will see recruiters increasingly turning to people analytics and smart algorithms for information to substantiate their decisions. The future of recruitment is no longer going to be an exclusively human enterprise. It will be a blend of human and computer involvement, with the latter gaining ground every single day.

> If they wish to have increased agility, companies will be turning to agile talent at an increasing rate. This means they will increasingly need and want to verify their selections by doing predictive analysis. Large international businesses, Microsoft for instance, have already started to use smart and predictive algorithms to analyse who is successful at work, who should be promoted and, most importantly, why? The Redmond-based IT and software business still believes people analytics is in its infancy, but knows it shall grow at an exponential rate in the next few years. Analytics is serious business: one in every three employees of companies like Google and Microsoft has a background in analytics.

Artificial intelligence, data analytics and virtual reality can all help you to delve deeper into the behaviour of candidates. Placing candidates in a realistic situation during the selection process is one way to test their behaviour in a range of circumstances and on all sorts of job-related issues – immunity to stress, willingness to collaborate, flexibility, customer-based mindset and learning agility, for example.

Holacracy and Agile Ways of Working – Hype or Happening?

Right now, holacracy (more commonly known as "self-organisation") and agile ways of working are very on-trend. I have noticed that virtually every single business that I am familiar with has begun to explore the principles of agile work, and is discussing the feasibility and benefits of implementing these principles. Fans of "agile" tend to sing its praises, particularly the level of commitment, flexibility, productivity, effectiveness and customer orientation. On the other hand, its critics say it is simply old wine in new wineskins and is likely to grow old soon enough. Neither of these stances rings true. A study done by *Harvard Business Review* has, in fact, found that this way of working might help businesses to adapt to the world in flux, though most of them are unlikely to apply agile principles throughout their whole organisation. It seems more prescient to opt for a considered and gradual approach. For many and even most businesses there might be issues and areas of expertise that allow for the swift adoption of the principles of agile work and holacracy. Other issues and areas will see an ongoing commitment to traditional ways of working.

My Vision and Definition of Agile Talent

Regardless of whether self-organisation and agile work conquer the corporate world, the speed and impact of technological change will have a disruptive effect on an unprecedented number of organisations. The only way to keep up is to adopt new ways of doing business.

My definition of agile talent on pages 20-21 does not necessarily involve people working in an agile setting within an organisation. In the first place, it applies to people who are capable of swiftly and efficiently adapting to evolving circumstances, and who can unlearn familiar patterns and maxims. If the hype of self-organising teams and agile ways of working were to blow over, the need to select agile talent will still remain strong.

Shifting and Evolving Criteria

The following list will give you an idea of the evolution of talent criteria through the years. On the left are those which were in the lead until recently, on the right are the criteria for selecting agile talent.

SKILLS
DEGREES **IQ**
RIGHT BRAIN FOCUS
EXPERIENCE
EQ **KNOWLEDGE**

SELECTION CRITERIA – TODAY AND THE PAST FEW YEARS

RIGHT BRAIN FOCUS
ANALYTICAL MIND
INTROSPECTION DETERMINATION
ADAPTABILITY
INSPIRATION **LEARNING**
REDUCE COMPLEXITY **AGILITY**
INTUITION
CREATIVITY WILLINGNESS TO
COLLABORATE
IQ, EQ & AQ
CURIOSITY **RESILIENCE**
STRONG NEED FOR ACHIEVEMENT
LEFT BRAIN FOCUS

KEY CRITERIA FOR SELECTING AGILE (FUTURE-PROOF) TALENT

Assemble the Best Possible Team

Computerised tools can help make cogent analyses on how complementary and diverse a team is. For this reason, you will want to carefully consider the selection of the whole team. In the future, recruiters will no longer be presented with just this question: "Find the best person for the job in *this* context". Instead, they will be requested to "assemble the very best and most mutually complementary team, which can best cope with the relevant challenges on the table".

"Those who are learning-agile know what to do when they don't know what to do. They know the questions to ask, the people to work with to find the answers they need and they are comfortable being uncomfortable."

JOHN T. DELANEY, HUFFINGTONPOST.COM (JULY 11, 2013)

Colin Lee, a Dutch scientist at Erasmus University's Rotterdam School of Management,* states that in the future algorithms will even be able to predict which candidates might succeed at jobs that do not even exist yet. Until that day comes, it makes sense for you to build a selection process that allows you to recruit future-proof talent yourself. The most important reason why you want to surround yourself with agile talent, is summed up perfectly by John Delaney:** "They know the questions to ask, the people to work with to find the answers they need and they are comfortable being uncomfortable."

---

* Charlotte van 't Wout (April 12, 2016). "Het algoritme weet of je geschikt bent." *NRC Handelsblad.*

** John T. Delaney (July 11, 2013). "The Most In-Demand 21st Century Business Skill." *The Huffington Post.*

FURTHER READING

BOOKS

- Viktor Mayer-Schönberger & Kenneth Cukier (2013). *Big Data. A Revolution That Will Transform How We Live, Work, and Think.* Eamon Dolan/Houghton Mifflin Harcourt.

ARTICLES

- Marc Andreessen (August 20, 2011). "Why Software is Eating the World." *The Wall Street Journal.*
- Ethan Bernstein, John Bunch, Niko Canner & Michael Lee (July/August 2016). "Beyond the Holacracy Hype." *Harvard Business Review.*
- Michael Chui, James Manyika & Mehdi Miremadi (November 2015). "Four Fundamentals of Workplace Automation." McKinsey.com.
- John T. Delaney (July 11, 2013). "The Most In-Demand 21st Century Business Skill: Learning Agility." *The Huffington Post.*
- Gerald C. Kane (April 7, 2015). "'People analytics' Through Super-Charged ID Badges." *Sloan Management Review.*
- Greg Lindsay (September 21, 2015). "HR Meets Data. How Your Boss Will Monitor You To Create The Quantified Workplace." *Fast Company Co. Exist.*
- TheAIGames.com (March 8, 2016). "How to Find and Assess Developers Through A.I. Games." Video, SlideShare.net.

APPENDIX 1
SCHMIDT AND HUNTER'S FINDINGS

PREDICTIVE VALIDITY FOR OVERALL JOB PERFORMANCE OF GENERAL MENTAL ABILITY (GMA) SCORES COMBINED WITH A SECOND PREDICTOR				
PERSONNEL MEASURE	VALIDITY (R)	MULTIPLE R	ADDITIONAL VALIDITY FROM ADDING A SECOND PREDICTOR	% INCREASE IN VALIDITY
GMA tests	.51			
Work samples	.54	.63	.12	24%
Interview (structured)	.51	.63	.12	24%
Job knowledge tests	.48	.58	.07	14%
Integrity tests	.41	.65	.14	27%
Interview (unstructured)	.38	.55	.04	8%
Assessment centres	.37	.53	.02	4%
Biographical data	.35	.52	.01	2%
Conscientiousness tests	.31	.60	.09	18%
Reference checks	.26	.57	.06	12%
Job experience (years)	.18	.54	.03	6%
Years of education	.10	.52	.01	2%
Interests	.10	.52	.01	2%
Graphology	.02	.51	.00	0%
Age	.01	.51	.00	0%

APPENDIX 2
FEEDBACK FORM

This appendix consists of a feedback form used for the position of Director of Marketing for one of our clients in the insurance business. The client was convinced – and rightly so – that the various criteria were not equally significant. As a result, we decided to add weighting to them, on a scale of one (least important for this position) to five (most important for this position).

Our insurance company client was knowledgeable about HR and experienced in search and recruitment. Not only could he effortlessly pinpoint the crucial criteria, he could define each selection factor in detail, showing a keen understanding of what the position required. Our team worked with the client on categorising the criteria into core selection factors and foundation factors (non-negotiable). In addition to these categories, we listed several obstacles that would be disqualifiers: regardless of how well candidates matched all the other criteria, these would immediately disqualify them from consideration. The form ultimately consisted of more than skills and experience. We added some key personality traits, including being a collaborative person and having an introspective nature. Next, we opted to add some criteria specific to the selection of future-proof talent to the form.

The final form then contains various elements aimed at agile or future-proof talent. These are not listed separately. Instead they have been blended into some of the five core selection factors, and the "obstacles" category.

	WEIGHTING	CANDIDATE'S SCORE
NAME OF CANDIDATE: **DATE:** **INTERVIEWER:**		
Senior marketeer This senior marketeer with wide experience in consultancy (healthcare is not essential) has a solid track record in managing proposals, marketing communications (transition to online, co-creation with customers), distribution marketing, brand management and reputation management. Demonstrable expertise and experience at the cusp of marketing and finance. An instant grasp of complicated calculations for insurance premiums is a given. He/she is sharply customer-oriented, both externally and internally.	**3**	
People manager An experienced people manager who breathes integrity, clarity and transparency in action and words. He/she is open to inputs from all angles, and can also make bold decisions. ("Now that I have heard all the options, this is my decision."). Furthermore, he/she can get people to do their utmost and is committed to creating the right atmosphere and the conditions for others to succeed. The people manager is a collaborative person, and an ardent connector. In no way a loner with an oversized ego, this person is instead someone who eagerly taps into the complementary dynamic of the team. He/she has capably and successfully held supervisory positions in large and complex organisations, with responsibility for 50+ employees. This person instantly imparts trust and can boost employee satisfaction.	**2**	
Deeply experienced in marketing, in both public and private sectors This person has more than a decade of business experience and marketing experience. He/she has worked at the cusp of both the public and private sectors, such as in the healthcare or pension fund sectors, public transport, or any other complex situation with a demonstrable public/private sector blend. This person senses that this position is firmly rooted in both these worlds, and approaches it accordingly.	**4**	
Passionate about healthcare This highly driven, dynamic and robust marketing expert is intrinsically motivated and committed to healthcare, with a raft of resilience and grit available when the going gets tough. Results are what counts, as does devotion to a healthier Netherlands. Has a strong social commitment, and does not shy from self-criticism. A stickler for quality and the need for continual improvement. An inspiration to others, this energetic, motivating, approachable person has a great sense of humour to boot.	**5**	

	WEIGHTING	CANDIDATE'S SCORE
Conceptual thinker with robust capacity for execution This person is a visionary strategist. As well as being capable of charting a course for marketing and company strategies, this person can easily translate strategy into operational steps and achieve results. Proven track record in implementation. An intensely curious person, someone who takes new circumstances on board right away, keen to understand them. Besides excelling in familiar situations, he/she has masses of learning agility and is practiced at adapting to the new and unfamiliar.	**5**	
Academically advanced and relevant experience The man/ woman we're seeking has a Master's degree or higher, coupled with substantial hands-on experience. Smart and quick-witted, he/she displays proficiency in abstract thinking, including a capacity for reflection.	FOUNDATION/ NON-NEGO-TIABLE	
Obstacles (disqualifier) which stand in the way of fulfilling the position Examples include a huge ego, loner-type behaviour, or lack of introspection.		
Additional remarks by the interviewer:		

APPENDIX 3
GLOSSARY

Agile talent Agility found in talented people. In this book, this refers to talented individuals who are able to swiftly adapt to new situations and altered circumstances, making themselves future-proof in the process.

Derailers Specific risks that might derail the candidate. The opposite of growth factors.

Disruptive innovation Innovation which disrupts the status quo in unforeseen ways.

Executive search Search and recruitment of very senior management positions, board members and supervisory boards.

Feedback form Form including the key criteria for a structured, criterion-based interview. In this case, the criteria play the part of an "umbrella" over the candidate's interview.

Minimum Viable Products An early, low-key version of a product, with the aim of assessing the product's viability and profitability. An MVP should require as little effort as possible, for maximum input from its users.

Onboarding Programme to provide new staff members (and management) with an ideal start in a new position, by showing them the ropes and introducing them to the company culture.

Optimisation algorithm An algorithm used to provide the best solution for problems, particularly those with a huge range of possible solutions. By implication, such a range means it would be unfeasible to try out every possible individual solution.

Peter Principle A concept in management theory which refers to the fact that staffers and management tend to be promoted up to the level of their own incompetence. Formulated by Laurence J. Peter and published in a book of that name in 1969.

Predictive validity Description of how valid predictions are produced by tests or assessments.

Retention The activities an organisation undertakes in order to retain talented individuals.

Search (assignment) The search assignment for which a search & recruitment agency, or executive search firm, must fill a particular position.

Silo thinking A tendency within an organisation not to think beyond a single department or business unit, for instance: marketing, sales, IT or customer service. Each department focuses on its own objectives, with little or no collaboration and communication between departments, or "silos".

Squads Small groups of staffers from a range of backgrounds, all working together on a shared project, objective or assignment. They constantly analyse and evaluate their ways of working, implementing short "bursts" of improvements.

Tribes The virtual umbrella over a distinct assignment or mission. Tribes consist of several squads.

ABOUT THE AUTHOR

Ralf Knegtmans is managing partner of the distinguished Leadership Consulting & Executive Search firm De Vroedt & Thierry. The company has a 40-year history and is based in Amsterdam. De Vroedt & Thierry is focused on the higher echelons of the market. Their client portfolio varies widely, ranging from public (international) companies to family-owned businesses, from private equity firms to NGOs, and includes several museums and other cultural organisations. For the past decade Knegtmans has – in addition to his everyday work – been a regular contributor to many leading Dutch media, both online and in print, including FD.nl, *De Financieele Telegraaf* and *Elsevier Magazine*. He has written several books, including: *Toptalent. De 9 universele criteria*, *Diversiteit als uitdaging. De zin en onzin van divers talent* and *Hoe word je CEO? Over competenties, persoonlijkheid en drijfveren*. He is also co-author of several books on strategic talent management. *Agile Talent* is the first of his books to be translated into English.

Speeches / presentations / guest lectures

On top of his everyday work at De Vroedt & Thierry, Knegtmans has become a recognised speaker in his field. He gives speeches and presentations in English as well as Dutch at conferences, companies and universities. If you would like to engage him as a speaker, on topics such as new leadership, agile top talent or meaningful diversity, please contact: his publisher Business Contact, Speakers Academy, Focus Conferences or the office of De Vroedt & Thierry at +31 20 662 76 27.

Special Edition

We offer you the option of having a special edition of the book, for a conference or seminar, or other special occasion, or as a gift for your clients. We can even have an edition with a bespoke cover according to your specifications. Please email us at ikee@atlascontact.nl

THANKS

Many hours of inspiring conversation helped to make this book what it is now. I spoke with the following people. They include CEOs, COOs, agile coaches and talents, HR managers, management gurus, authors of books on management, and other experts:

- Maarten van Beek, director Human Resources ING The Netherlands
- Willemijn Boskma, agile Scrum-coach advisor, Scrum Company
- George Bradt, executive onboarding specialist, columnist at Forbes.com, and author of several books, including *Onboarding. How to Get Your New Employees Up to Speed in Half the Time*
- Henk Breukink, founder of Executive Development Dialogue and supervisory board member
- Martin Danoestrastro, partner (agility) and MD Boston Consulting Group
- Ralph Hamers, CEO ING Group
- Raymond Hannes, co-founder and CEO Vita.io, and board member of PortXL
- Gabriëlle van Heteren, HR Business Consultant ABN AMRO Bank
- Frans van Houten, CEO Royal Philips NV
- Nick Jue, chairman and CEO ING The Netherlands
- Rina Joosten-Rabou, co-founder and CCO Seedlink Technologies
- Jetske van Kilsdonk-ten Kate, HR manager ING Retail Bank
- Sander Klous, partner Big Data Analytics KPMG and professor Big Data Ecosystems University of Amsterdam
- Bart Kollau, chief Feedback Office and co-founder TruQu
- Jacques Kuyf, interim manager, supervisory board member and partner De Vroedt & Thierry
- Frank van Luijk, assessment psychologist and leadership expert
- Kevin O'Donnell, director Business Communications, Cornerstone International Group, Beijing Office
- Ylva Poelman, bionica and innovations expert, author of *De natuur als uitvinder*
- Nancy Powers Koleda, consultant De Vroedt & Thierry
- Quintin Schevernels, investor in HR technology, author of *Suits & Hoodies*
- Bart Schlatmann, COO ING The Netherlands
- Judith Schulp, Lexence Advocaten
- Feike Sijbesma, CEO & Chairman Managing Board DSM

- Henk Jan Smit, partner KPMG Advisory N.V.
- Fons Trompenaars, leadership guru and author of several books, including *Riding the Waves of Culture* (with Charles Hampden-Turner)